Featherstone

A PRACTICAL GUIDE TO
Nature-Based Practice

NIKI BUCHAN

Featherstone
An imprint of Bloomsbury Publishing Plc

50 Bedford Square
London
WC1B 3DP
UK

1385 Broadway
New York
NY 10018
USA

www.bloomsbury.com

Bloomsbury is a registered trademark of Bloomsbury Publishing Plc

Text © Niki Buchan 2016

Photographs © Niki Buchan
Photographs p76, 95, 97 © Clare Nugent
Some photographs were taken while employed by Inspired EC
Additional photographs © Shutterstock

British Library Cataloguing-in-Publication Data
A catalogue record for this book is available from the British Library.

ISBN:
PB 978-1-4729-3835-0
ePDF 978-1-4729-3838-1

Library of Congress Cataloging-in-Publication Data
A catalogue record for this book is available from the Library of Congress.

1 3 5 7 9 10 8 6 4 2

Printed and bound in India by Replika Pvt Ltd.

This book is produced using paper that is made from wood grown in managed, sustainable forests. It is
natural, renewable and recyclable. The logging and manufacturing processes conform to the environmental
regulations of the country of origin.

To view more of our titles please visit www.bloomsbury.com

Acknowledgements
Thank you to the children for allowing me to share in their enthusiasm and joy of wild nature.

Thank you to my parents, Sybe and Annemarie Bakker, who allowed me the freedom to roam and to
explore wild nature. It is only as an adult that I realise the true value of this trust.

Thank you to my husband, David, and children, David, Stuart, Caitlin and Martin who put up with my
desire to wander and wonder in nature and to photograph what amazes me. Thank you for your continued
patience and support.

Thank you to Barney Rivers and Ruth Siems of Teaching Solutions and Helen Diamond of Bloomsbury
Publishing for believing in me. To Clare Nugent and Sarah MacQuarrie, friends and mentors, who
contributed chapter 7. To Juliet Robertson and Wendy Lee for their continuing support and kind words. To
family and friends who supported me.

Thank you to all the contributors who so generously shared their personal journeys, and a very special
thank you to all the children and families who shared their photographs and thoughts; without them a
book about UK practice would not have been possible.

Contents

Foreword

A *Practical Guide to Nature-Based Practice* is a practical guide to taking children beyond the walls of the traditional outdoor space and into local places with a sense of wildness – be this woodland, beaches, a nearby park or open moorland. The author, Niki Buchan, is a highly-respected early years consultant whose breadth and depth of experiences spans almost four decades and three continents.

Niki grew up in rural South Africa, where the breathtaking scenery and freedom to roam gave her a unique and precious childhood. In her 20s and 30s she established two nature-based nurseries, before moving to the UK with her Scottish husband, David, and four children, where she continued to develop her outdoor philosophy, helped to set up and manage two Nature Kindergartens and discovered her passion and talent for photography. Several years ago, seeking a warmer climate and new challenges, Niki and David moved to Australia, where Niki now works as an educational trainer and consultant. She remains active and up-to-date with UK developments through her annual trips to the UK to facilitate study visits and speak at conferences.

This book was originally published in Australia as *Children in Wild Nature* to illustrate and celebrate the Australian and New Zealand nature-based early years practice that has emerged over the past five years within both countries. It provides practical illustrations of the benefits of children spending frequent and regular time in a familiar natural environment where they can return time after time. Niki articulates the necessity for children to have free play in nature. This is put in the context of how adults, through their observations and reflections can effectively meet the needs of their children and provide a solid education.

In this edition, Niki has adapted the book for UK early years educators, providing a useful blend of background, research, guidance and practical suggestions within the context of our own landscape, culture and curricula. The case studies are deliberately broad in terms of the location and practice. They are a celebration of the diversity of nature-based pedagogy emerging throughout the UK.

From my own work on developments such as the Forestry Commission Scotland's Forest Kindergarten Project, I have witnessed first-hand the positive impact of enabling young children to access and experience playing in woodland, beaches and other greenspace. Children's confidence grows as they repeatedly return to a known space. The changing seasons provide a context for ongoing discussions and explorations. An icy patch in winter turns to mud in the spring. By summer it has dried up and in autumn is covered in leaves. Children's stamina improves as they develop the muscles and coordination needed to negotiate uneven surfaces and to walk distances that often surprise adults. They learn how to read the weather and the environment and become better able to make decisions about what to wear and where to play. The uncertainty of life beyond a boundary fence of a designated outdoor space provides opportunities to learn real-world skills such as road safety and make decisions when faced with challenges such as encountering an injured wild animal.

In our rapidly-changing world, we have a responsibility to our children to provide a positive legacy and a secure foundation for their future. *A Practical Guide to Nature-Based Practice* demonstrates a sustainable and rights-based approach where adventures in nature provide valuable learning experiences that prepare children for life and living.

**Juliet Robertson, Education Consultant,
Creative STAR Learning**

Chapter 1

Introducing nature-based practice

What is nature-based practice?

Nature-based practice is the skill of working with children in and with nature. It is a philosophy, a way of being, ideally practised indoors and outdoors. Children have a natural affinity with and connection to nature; and throughout this book I share the researched benefits of children being outdoors, preferably in a wild, natural environment. It therefore makes sense that such natural spaces are ideal environments to holistically nurture children, to allow them to grow, to develop, to learn and to thrive. Teaching outdoors in wild nature is very different to teaching indoors, and may require a mind-shift for some practitioners. This pedagogy of being in nature with children, where children learn and develop with the often unique learning opportunities offered in nature is valued by practitioners skilled in practising in wild nature.

What is wild nature?

Wild nature is nature as it is found, with fallen sticks, washed-up shells and opportunities for the unpredictable. These might be spaces where there are still pathways and signs, but nature in its natural state is maintained. They do not necessarily need to be large spaces – and may be a natural space next to a sports field, on a vacant plot or in a botanical garden.

Wild nature is not nature that has been tidied up, cleaned, prepared or processed. Many children's playgrounds with only man-made static equipment and manicured gardens do not allow for the joy of nature-based practice.

Luke Addison of Riverside Cottage Nursery, a nursery that offers children the freedom to roam and explore the large natural environment, comments on the stinging nettles found naturally in their Upper Woodland site:

> *This area is FULL of stinging nettles and thistles throughout the summer months. The adults make very little effort to control these although the children sometimes do their best to remove them from specific areas if they are becoming annoying. We have never really thought anything of this but without exception, visitors from local state-run nurseries remark on this and can't believe we haven't weeded them out.*

While wild nature may contain minor natural hazards; children learn to negotiate these through knowledge and experience (this will be explored further in Chapter 5).

The *Wild About Play* Research Report identified wild spaces as green spaces that may be completely natural as well as spaces, such as urban parks, where there are also artificial elements. They further defined such spaces as having no specific shape, size or natural elements:

> *Wild spaces are: country lanes, hedgerows, woodland, city farms, grassland, beaches, heathland, gardens, rivers, shrubs, verges, ponds, fields, hills, parks, trees, farmland, sand dunes, village greens, muddy hollows.*
>
> *Maudsley, 2004*

Don't feel restricted. The children of Urafirth Primary School, Shetland Islands, were excited to share their own forest and demonstrate their tree-climbing skills. This was all the more exciting because there are not many trees on the Shetland Islands.

A short history of nature-based practice

Learning with nature has been part of the history of Western European education since the 18th century; Rousseau, Froebel, McMillan and Montessori all advocated the benefits of learning with nature through play in a sensory environment.

The nature-practice model initiative originated in Scandinavia and the Nordic countries where children don't attend formal schooling until the age of seven. Until then children learn through play, and nature is part of the everyday culture and experience. The natural environment is seen as a teacher, play is valued and the attitude to risk is positive. Pedagogy in these countries sees formal education as only one part of the experience of the child's development. The first record of a Danish nature school is from 1950 and currently over 10% of Danish preschools see the natural world as central to children's early development

There is a long tradition of craftwork in European education with the use of real tools and exploring the use of natural materials using skills handed down through generations. Many of these are not commonly introduced in UK early childhood environments possibly due to the perception of risks.

In 1993 a group of nursery nurses and lecturers from Bridgwater College in Somerset, visited Denmark to explore the outdoor forest centres and returned to establish their own Forest School programme. They are recognised as the pioneers of the Forest School concept in the UK.

There are a number of different, valuable models of nature-based practice in the UK:

✿ **Forest Schools** developed into weekly sessions in a forest environment run by qualified Forest School level 3 practitioners. In this approach, children have access to a forest site for two to three hours per week often over a six-week period.

✿ **Nature Kindergartens/Nursery Schools** where young children (not yet of school-going age) spend prolonged periods of time playing with children of mixed ages in wild nature on a daily basis.. These are run by qualified early childcare teachers – some may have additional qualifications in working with children outdoors.

✿ **Nature Schools** are schools where school-aged children spend prolonged periods of time in wild nature on a daily basis. These are run by qualified teachers, some of whom may have additional qualifications in working with children outdoors.

✿ **Eco-schools** take a holistic, participatory approach to learning for sustainability. Some may follow a nature-based practice programme.

According to the 2016 Care Inspectorate document: *My World Outdoors*, The Secret Garden in Fife became the first full-time, outdoor-based nursery in the UK when it was registered in 2008. 'These new outdoor-based forest nurseries follow in the footsteps of the pioneers of Scottish early learning and childcare.'

It is particularly exciting that the Scottish Care Inspectorate's approach to outdoor-based nurseries is supportive; they have encouraged the development of a range of outdoors-only provision since that first application to register a nursery running solely in a woodland without traditional premises.

There is a big difference educationally and experientially between children accessing a space once a week for two hours over a six-week period and children accessing a space every day for many hours all year round. Apart from the continuity of experiences, the more exposure children have to nature, the greater the benefits.

> *Nature alleviates the impact of life stress on children and helps them deal with adversity. The greater the amount of nature exposure, the greater the benefits.*
>
> Wells & Evans, 2003

Children, including babies, at Dunblane Nature Kindergarten in Scotland have access to real-life experiences such as cooking on a fire. Curiosity drives this little person to open up the foil enclosing potatoes waiting to be baked on the fire.

Children exploring white sandy beaches on the Shetland Islands, challenging the waves and having to face the consequences of wet clothing on a chilly summer's day.

Why is nature-based practice so important?

Many adults have memories of being free to roam, to explore the rivers, the beach and the forests. Such memories, together with the well-researched negative consequences to children of not having contact with nature have led to a growing movement among concerned educators, academics and parents to address this imbalance that denies children the right and privilege of experiencing so much of what the UK outdoors truly has to offer.

According to William Bird's research on children and nature, children have progressively lost the right to roam freely from their homes within four generations. There now appears to be a growing realisation and desire among parents to allow their children adventurous childhoods, and this desire is fuelling the growth in nature-based settings. I believe it is the duty of every childcare provider to offer children extended periods of time outside the constraints of walled classrooms and into wild nature:

> *...increasingly the role of registered early learning and childcare services is to proactively ensure that children have a range of experiences outdoors, from the service's own outdoor play area, local parks and further afield.*
>
> Care Inspectorate, 2016

Wendy Lee, co-director of the Early Childhood Learning and Assessment National Exemplar Project Kei Tua o te Pae, New Zealand, so rightly states that

> *children need to be involved in 'wild' spaces. They need dynamic and complex outdoor environments and opportunities for risk and challenge – to play with abandon – to have first-hand experiences. A place where there is: adventure, delight, laughter, daring and joy!*

Large open spaces at Riverside Cottage Nursery allow children to lead the way, to go on an adventure, with that perception of freedom which is so often lacking in the current climate of fear.

Outings into wild nature

Different wild nature experience models are emerging, which is exciting and encouraging. Many are still initial, exploratory visits, but through reflection and evaluation many practitioners are starting to adopt a more nature-based approach to their practice.

Invitations to explore further come in many different forms. An inviting sign and track with a hidden destination offers children of Brae Primary School, Shetland Islands, an invitation to explore further, beyond the visible equipment.

Current models

Current models of getting children out into the wild vary depending on philosophy, knowledge and opportunity. Some common models are:

✿ occasional outings away from the setting, often annually or quarterly

✿ weekly outings, usually for two to three hours, often over a set time period, for example six weeks

✿ weekly or twice-weekly outings, for half a day or a full day, throughout the year

✿ daily access for shorter periods of time, often within the playground setting

✿ daily access for prolonged periods of time throughout the year.

Each of these models can also have a number of variations:

✿ limitations on the numbers and ages of children

✿ the allocated natural space in which the children can roam freely

✿ the opportunities children have access to and the activities offered

✿ the adult involvement, including the freedom, directions or instructions given to the children

✿ the type of resources or equipment available to the children.

At Dunblane Nature Kindergarten the natural philosophy is integrated; children have access to a range of open-ended natural resources in the playground, as well as indoors.

Working towards an integrated philosophy

Some centres, with the best of intentions, have set up experiences for children with many guidelines and rules, where the current structured indoor practice gets transferred into the garden or wild nature and where children end up returning to a largely artificial environment. Ideally we would like to work towards a more integrated approach, a naturalistic philosophy that touches every aspect of children's experiences – a place that incorporates community, naturalistic indoor and outdoor space as well as access to wild nature, and where the philosophy and practice in each space does not change, although the experiences may differ.

This is a journey, so opportunities will be different, and for some, easy access to a forest or wild nature space may be limited. A naturalistic philosophy is achievable even in a challenging inner-city playground.

At the beginning of the journey, a nature-based centre may be one where:

✿ a number of natural resources have been introduced into the indoor environment

✿ the outdoor garden space has a number of natural resources such as logs, water and sand

✿ children have some access to a natural space beyond the gate or in the playground during excursions

✿ children and parents are consulted on a number of issues relating to them

✿ children's interests are valued and evidence of sustainable practice is evident.

During the journey a nature-based centre may be one where:

✿ the indoor space has predominantly natural, open-ended resources

✿ the outdoor garden space has a range of natural resources and practitioners are starting to appreciate the importance of children being allowed to take risks

✿ children have weekly access to a wild space, possibly beyond the gate, and are starting to build a connection to such spaces

✿ children, parents and practitioners are respected and consulted on a wide range of issues related to the centre

✿ practitioners follow children's interest and are starting to embrace risk and challenge. Opportunities are developmentally appropriate and sustainability is becoming more embedded.

A fully integrated nature-based centre is one where:

✿ the indoor environment is a homely, calm and uncluttered natural space filled with open-ended natural opportunities

✿ there is a calm naturalistic outdoor garden space offering opportunities for risk and challenge

✿ there is a strong connection to the local community and environment, where regular, prolonged periods of time in 'wild' natural spaces are valued and supported

✿ an ethos and philosophy of genuine caring, consultation and respect between children, families, staff and management exists

✿ the practice of deep respect, developmentally appropriate opportunities, working in 'nature time' at the child's pace, embracing risk and challenge exists. Embedded sustainability is offered consistently throughout.

Reassure families that children WILL get muddy and that this is OK.

NATURE-BASED PRACTICE INDOORS

The indoor spaces reflect the naturalistic ethos of integrated nature-based practice. Natural floors are used as they are easy to clean, allowing children to access the indoor spaces feely, without necessarily removing their outdoor clothing or shoes. Open-ended and natural resources, such as wooden blocks, pine cones and stones are freely available. Natural light, uncluttered spaces, table cloths, pot plants and quality furniture create a homely feel and show respect for children and practitioners.

Dunblane Nature Kindergarten uses a combination of processed and natural wooden furniture indoors.

Natural light, moving shadows, furniture in neutral colours and flowers on the table invite children into this indoor space as they freely transition between the indoors and outdoors at Boldon Nursery School - Outdoor Nursery.

Snuggling up for a personal story next to the wood-burning stove at Riverside Cottage Nursery while others choose to continue playing.

Boldon Nursery School offers a children's kitchen complete with fridge and a mini stove that really works within their natural indoor space. This demonstrates the adult's value and belief in the children's capabilities both indoors and outdoors.

What does nature-based practice look like in the UK today?

One of the goals of writing this book was to raise awareness of the many settings currently embracing nature-based practice as well as the diversity of practice found in the UK and internationally; from the Forest School model, where children access natural spaces one morning a week for a set number of weeks, to Nature Kindergartens and Nature Schools where the natural philosophy and way of working with children is embedded throughout the setting on a daily basis. It is often through having such an awareness of like-minded visions and practice nearby that change happens.

No book about nature-based practice should be without the voices of the many practitioners, families and children who are already on this exciting journey. With this in mind, as research for this book, a questionnaire was sent out to ten very different settings across the UK using different models of nature-based practice in their settings. In most cases practitioners had to push the boundaries, and stand up for the rights of the children. Not always an easy journey, but if practitioners do not stand up for the rights of the child... who will?

> *Every teacher, every caregiver, holds in his or her hands the power to shape a child's entire future.*
>
> Schiller, 2009

Throughout the book you will find tips, advice and real examples taken directly from practitioners and settings, many of which I visited as research for this book. As well as this there are detailed case studies on each different setting.

Setting 1 Child First, Northampton, England

Practitioner interviewed: Angela Green, manager

Description of the setting: A centre set in three acres of woodland for children aged zero to four. Also offers Forest School sessions for groups of eight children, aged three years and above, lasting three hours. Resources include: vast open spaces, mud kitchen, a large vegetable garden, a wild wooded area, swings, outdoor eating area and a sleeping hut. Children spend extended periods of time outdoors daily.

Setting 2 Riverside Cottage Nursery, Bathgate, Scotland

Practitioner interviewed: Luke Addison, manager

Description of the setting: Riverside Cottage Nursery offers day care of children (fully private) including after-school and holiday club care. 15-20 children attend during the day with an additional 10-15 after-schoolers arriving at 3.45pm. Resources include: a dog to walk, outdoor toilet, outdoor classroom, large organic allotment, wooded area with climbing equipment and mud kitchen as well as a 'wilder' woodland with climbing trees and a fire pit. Children have free-flow access to these spaces all day. They also have regular access to wild nature beyond the nursery grounds: a river, farm fields, woodland and a 161 hectare nature reserve.

The outdoor classroom allows children to shelter and warm up while retaining the outdoor feeling.

Wild nature spaces without man-made structures offer another 'wild' dimension to children's experiences.

Setting 3 Home educator, Shetland Islands

Practitioner interviewed: Alex Purbrick, mother and home educator

Description of the setting: Alex has three children aged five, seven and nine who she educates at home and has taken into wild spaces from birth. Their house is surrounded by large natural open countryside which they try to go out into every day for varying amounts of time depending on the season. They have access to beaches, woods, heather moorlands, prehistoric rock formations, ancient ruins, peat hills and a quarry.

Each of the children have their own particular interests and passions; Alex likes them to find their own unique ways of connecting with nature.

Setting 4 Dream Days, Northumberland, England

Practitioner interviewed: Kimberley Wilford, creator

Description of the setting: Kimberley cares for six children aged from nine months to school age within her home. The children have access to the garden and wild spaces throughout the day. The garden has fruit trees, a growing patch, a stove, a water pump, bricks, and outside the garden they also have access to a river, embankment and a park.

Even the youngest children are able to explore in a hands-on, sensorial manner while dressed appropriately for the weather and the opportunity.

Setting 5 Dunblane Nature Kindergarten, Dunblane, Scotland

Practitioner interviewed: Steven White, project co-ordinator

Description of the setting: The centre offers wrap-around, full day care for 95 children aged from six months to five years from 7.30am until 6.30pm. It is situated in the centre of the town of Dunblane and children have access to the outdoor spaces daily for as long as they want. Resources include a playground with a fire, a garden space (with a sandpit and flower beds) and an outdoor classroom. Children also have access to green spaces in and around the town of Dunblane including streams, rivers, hills, scrub and wildlife.

The outdoor space has been converted into a natural playground with real grass, a fire pit, wooden logs and a large sand pit.

Setting 6 — The Orchard Nature Nursery, Dumfries, Scotland

Practitioner interviewed: Kim Bannister, owner/manager

Description of the setting: The Orchard Nature Nursery offers full day care to 35 children aged from zero to five years old. The children have access to varying wild spaces every day where they can stay all day if they choose to do so. Spaces include the garden which has no pre-made structure, just loose parts like tyres, bread crates, guttering and wood cut offs, the grounds of a private estate which include a large green space, rock garden and waterfall, and they also have access to a local forest and beach.

Children have regular access to the local beach which offers a whole new dimension to their already rich natural experiences. Scrambling across the rough rocks needs children to be good self-risk assessors. Child's comment, 'We know how to keep safe'.

Setting 7 — Nature Nurture, Aberdeen, Scotland

Practitioner interviewed: Terri Harrison, project co-ordinator, early intervention

Description of the setting: Nature Nurture offers vulnerable children including children and young people from families affected by substance misuse, alcohol abuse, domestic violence, abusive relationships, neglect and poverty access to the nature spaces once a week. The children aged two to five years old, five to eight years old and eight to eleven years old stay for half a day during the term time, while during the school holidays whole day sessions are run. Each session is attended by ten children and they have access to woodland areas via farmlands, fields, riversides, meadows and parkland.

Children are provided with appropriate clothing and are eager to spend time in the natural environment in all weathers.

Setting 8 — Alfreton Nursery School, Alfreton, England

Practitioner interviewed: Angela Stanton, headteacher

Description of the setting: At Alfreton Local Authority Nursery School two sessions are run each week: one in the morning and one in the afternoon for different groups of children. Each Forest School session lasts for two and a half hours and is attended by 12 children aged three and four years old. Every child in the nursery is given the opportunity to attend at least 20 sessions during their time in nursery. Resources include an on-site Forest School including woodland, mud pie kitchen, log circle with fire-building equipment, a permanent shelter and feeding stations, as well as a larger field including trees, a greenhouse, allotment, new habitat spaces and willow structures.

A natural tunnel created out of living willow, changes with the seasons.

Setting 9   Abacus Filton Hill Preschool, Bristol, England

Practitioner interviewed: Annette Parsons, manager

Description of the setting: Abacus Filton Hill is situated within the primary school and open during term time. It caters for 20 children every day aged from two to five years old. The children access wild nature every day for at least two and a half hours, including woods, brooks, steep banks and hills, streams, rivers, fields and wide, open spaces. They also have access to natural and man-made loose parts and water.

Children may choose to take open-ended resources such as ropes into the water to extend their play.

Setting 10   Boldon Nursery School: Outdoor Nursery, South Tyneside, England

Practitioner interviewed: Sue Stokoe, Headteacher

Description of the setting: There are 48 children aged three to four years old in each session and they have continuous access to the garden and wild spaces within the setting. Children who attend full days (40%) can choose to be outdoors for six hours a day while others who attend for three hours daily can spend all that time outdoors. They have access to on-site resources including a wild space with trees, shrubs, flowers, wild plants, fire pit, mud and puddles, as well as access to a local burn (park) with a stream, trees, a copse, hills and flat landscapes, and the beach with a lighthouse, sand dunes and rock pools.

Negotiating a wet, slippery log is excitingly challenging. Every child approaches this in a way that is developmentally appropriate for that individual child.

Putting it into practice

It is important to have a vision, to reflect and analyse, recognise and overcome challenges, to identify any adaptations required and then create a model that best works for you. Every journey will be different and in this book you will:

- ✿ learn more about the nature-based practice approach and the benefits it offers those children in your care (Chapter 2)

- ✿ be encouraged to consider the vision for your setting (Chapter 3)

- ✿ be provided with practical guidance on implementing a nature-based practice approach in your setting (Chapter 4)

- ✿ explore possible challenges and risks involved and be given practical strategies to overcome or manage them (Chapter 5)

- ✿ discover lots of creative ideas and opportunities you can use with your children in a natural setting (Chapter 6)

- ✿ be encouraged to consider a more theory-based, academic analysis of nature-based practice (Chapter 7)

- ✿ meet some of the practitioners who use a nature-based practice approach and have kindly shared their own unique journey (throughout the book).

The benefits for your children

> *Exposure to natural environments improves children's cognitive development by improving their awareness, reasoning and observational skills.*
>
> Pyle, 2002

Why take children into wild nature? Why nature-based practice?

Simply being outside in the fresh air is beneficial; add to that the ability to actively explore nature first hand, and the benefits increase dramatically. This is when we see children flourish, and for some children, who struggle within a classroom or playground, the change is transformational and often life-changing.

Children have a remarkable ability to adapt the way they move to accommodate the conditions, whether it be cautiously exploring a snowy slippery slope, increasing their pace and playing energetically on a cold day or slowing down and selecting cooler spaces to play on a hot day. Nature challenges all at an appropriate level. To negotiate a fallen tree, the competent climber scrambles to the highest point while another child climbs on a small log, each achieving that 'I did it' moment that comes with celebrating achievement.

There are huge benefits to nature-based practice for all children, whatever their ability or age. They are outlined below in more detail, and include the opportunity to have a childhood, to play, to make decisions and face responsibility, to explore new and familiar spaces, to learn with nature, to develop a nature identity and to realise the importance of the natural environment.

Balancing on the rocks to negotiate the stream takes skill and practice. Some choose to crawl along and celebrate their achievement as enthusiastically as those hopping from rock to rock.

NBP in action

CONTEXTUAL LEARNING IN NATURE

A 13-year-old boy at Spirit of Play Community School in Australia selected and broke four small twigs into equal lengths. He placed them into the sand with a V-shaped fork at the top, balancing small sticks into the V pieces of bark to form the roof. Younger children collected natural materials. Collaboratively, a pathway of tiny stones, trees and gardens, a fire pit with mini sitting logs and four small wire people were created. After 45 minutes of intense involvement by the boy, the play started to wind down.

'Wouldn't it be nice to have this shelter in the forest for the children?' I commented and then moved away. This was the scaffolding or intentional teaching opportunity offered by the adult. The boy fetched a tape measure and took accurate measurements of the structure – both in centimetres and inches – modelling this process to the younger children.

After more than an hour playing, he took a photograph and sent it to his friends. This is the 'I did it' moment that comes with facing a challenge and successfully completing it without adult interference. At the end of the session he removed the little wire people, leaving only the natural materials.

Was he playing? Was he involved? Was learning happening? Was he having fun? Yes, most certainly. What learning could be observed in the following areas: maths, science, engineering, technology, language, literacy, sustainability, emotional and social, knowledge of the world, and possible other areas too?

Valuing children's free play

Play, learning and development are all interconnected and facilitated by a high-quality environment. The link between play, learning and academic achievement has been well documented. In nature-based practice children's free play is valued, encouraged and often documented for families and children.

> *Play provides the active explorations that assists in building and strengthening brain pathways shaping the structure. Play creates a brain that has increased flexibility and improved potential for learning later in life.*
>
> Lester & Russell, *Play for a Change*, 2008

Throwing stones into water is an age-old natural 'drive' for young and old. At Riverside Cottage Nursery this young boy is unconsciously developing muscle control and scientific concepts through his play.

Nature-based practice values children's play and recognises that learning occurs when children are playing naturally. Sadly, practitioners may need to advocate the benefits of nature-based practice through the learning and development that occurs as not everybody 'gets it'.

Children, like all young mammals, learn by playing, and the more they have to learn, the more they need to play. There is a great similarity internationally in not just how children play but also in what they play. Chasing games, risky play, pushing and shoving, hide-and-seek are universal, as is building dens, although the language, material and structure may be different.

Free play in nature is self-motivating and engaging. Children will naturally explore many scientific, technological, engineering and mathematical concepts as they play and construct with natural found objects.

Free play and learning

Is learning play or is play learning? Do we learn through play or play to learn? To me these questions are irrelevant; play is what children do, play is what childhood is about, play is what children have a right to. It just so happens that play is also about:

- decision making
- sharing
- making friends
- getting along
- negotiating
- making and following rules
- solving problems
- reaching consensus

- regulating emotions
- exercising self-control
- developing interests
- mathematics
- science
- language
- history
- cultural concepts

and so much more!

Young children at Nature Nurture have minimal resources outdoors. The resources available are familiar and open-ended to stimulate imagination and investigation. Bamboo pieces and water provide endless play and learning opportunities as well as increasing children's well-being.

Defining free play

There are numerous definitions for free play. According to Shipley (2008) it is enjoyable and may include frustrations, fear and challenges. It is symbolic, often pretend and has meaning to the child. It is active – physical, verbal or mental – and requires action with people, resources, ideas or the environment. Play is always voluntary; children can choose to opt in or opt out. It is process-orientated with no end or goal planned and lastly it is self-motivating and does not need a reward; the play itself is the reward.

My favourite definition of play came from a four-year-old boy. When asked 'I wonder what play is?' he thought about it and responded 'Play is when adults stop telling me what to do!'

True 'free play' is hard to achieve, but reducing constraints such as limitations on time, space and resources is a big first step. Activities such as ballet, football and board games, while beneficial when played appropriately, are not child-initiated free play. Nature-based practice as suggested in this book is as close as I have seen children in supervised care playing freely.

Many of the benefits that follow are linked to the benefits offered by 'free play' in a nature-based setting.

Children at Riverside Cottage Nursery have very clearly indicated to the adults that they are not needed or wanted in the upper woodland space.

Experiencing childhood

Childhood should be a time of joy, of freedom away from the pressures of adult life. Childhood is also a time for children to seek and make meaning of their world or at times, to just BE. Sadly, currently childhood may also be a time of great stress and anxiety.

Nature-based practice supports a range of quality experiences in nature for children of all ages with the belief that children are entitled to a high-quality childhood. Many of these experiences are not possible indoors or even in an 'artificial' playground with static man-made equipment and artificial, leafless and stickless surfaces. In nature, children have access to space, they encounter many living creatures and experience true adventure including sitting around a fire. They experience fun, autonomy, responsibility and are building memories for life.

Finding, identifying, picking and eating the sweet berries found in the wild are fond childhood memories these children at Nature Nurture are likely to remember.

Children as the decision-makers

Children have the right to be involved and to be heard in matters that affect them.

> *Education should consider the children's perspective, give children a voice, listen to them and take them seriously.*
>
> UN Convention on the Rights of the Child, 1989

As mentioned above, play in nature-based practice is self-initiated and spontaneous, giving children ownership. They become the designers and creators of their environment: building dens, stacking stones, decorating sandcastles and breaking them down again. Practitioners who are often 'obsessive tidy-uppers' indoors do not feel the urge to clear away sticks, stones and shells allowing children to come back to continue their play.

Children are directors as well as initiators of their actions and investigations in play. They make choices, they know what they are doing although they may not always correctly anticipate the consequences. They are responsible for their decisions.

Sitting high up in a tree, just 'being' with nobody questioning his motives or cautioning him against perceived dangers creates valuable memories.

Revisiting a den built at Nature Nurture. As the designers and creators, children have ownership and will revisit such spaces to reflect on their experiences and learning as well as adjusting or repairing as they deem necessary.

Taking responsibility

Children are encouraged to take responsibility and face consequences, both the positive and not so positive. A child might take a calculated risk, run across the sand dunes, fall face-first down the dune, splutter and then continue climbing and running until they have reached the highest point – and we can share this celebration with a smile or a thumbs-up, the fall and sandy face forgotten. A duty of care means ensuring that the hazards are visible and risks acceptable, not shielding children from life experiences and lessons.

Playing in the stream some children at Riverside Cottage choose to walk in deeper than the height of their boots and then have to face the consequences of walking back with wet clothing.

Exploring new spaces

Exploring new spaces is not merely taking a walk along a path. It means stepping off the well-trodden path and finding a place to settle and explore. Children often choose a base – a log, a little hill or a hollow in the landscape – somewhere they can come back to, where they can leave their water bottles and their treasures. Adults may decide on the main base where they have an overview of the space. Some children may initially feel apprehensive; for them having a base as an initial starting point offers a sense of security. They might choose to remain close until they feel safe before extending their area of exploration.

Children's prior experience plays a role here, and those who have experienced a variety of spaces outdoors are likely to be less reserved than others for whom accessing outdoor spaces is a less regular feature of their childhood. The same applies to the adults working with them.

Coming back to familiar spaces

Given the choice, children will often want to go back to a familiar site again and again and again! As their confidence increases, their explorations expand. They explore new concepts, investigate and compare the new with the old. They become aware of changes that occur when they are not present – changes brought about by the seasons or by humans or animals. They consider such familiar spaces as theirs, taking ownership and becoming protective of the now-familiar fauna and flora.

By visiting the same space over time, children don't need the same initial settling-in period. They are able to continue where they left off, to find familiar bugs and plants and previously played with materials.

A rustic shelter forms the base at another of the Nature Nurture sites often used by the younger children.

The base for these children at one of the Nature Nurture sites is a natural clearing in the forest, next to the stream where a campfire is lit. From here children can explore freely while being sensitively observed and monitored by the adults.

Nature is a natural educator

> *Do not train children to learn by force and harshness, but direct them to it by what amuses their minds, so that you may be better able to discover with accuracy the peculiar bent of the genius of each.*
>
> Plato

Plato, like Howard Gardner, believed that we learn best through our interests. Children naturally have a strong connection to nature. By two years of age they enjoy discovering a spider hiding at the centre of its web, or finding a puddle to jump in.

Edward Wilson (1984) refers to this as biophilia. The biophilia hypothesis suggests that there is an instinctive bond between human beings and other living things. Nature-based practice harnesses this natural affiliation and supports the most natural learning pathway for all children.

For many children, wild nature outings might be their only real experience with a natural environment where they can experience nature on nature's terms. They will return to a setting with artificial surfaces, adult structure and plastic toys.

For others, the outing is a natural extension of what occurs on a day-to-day basis. The goal would always be to transfer and align nature-based practice with the ethos of the whole setting to truly offer an integrated nature-based programme throughout.

Dunblane Nature Kindergarten's indoor spaces reflect how the natural ethos is followed indoors through a combination of open-ended wild natural logs and crafted resources made out of wood and felt.

Babies at Dunblane Nature Kindergarten are appropriately dressed for the weather and the conditions, enabling them to freely explore the natural space around them.

The outdoor environment at Dunblane Nature Kindergarten reflects the same natural ethos with children having access to open-ended resources such as metal containers, tyres, water and planks of wood.

The philosophy of nature-based practice is followed during transition at Into the Woods Outdoor Nursery, with even the youngest child trusted and seen as capable and competent to take the lead in moving to a different familiar space.

Benefits in the words of our practitioners

The actual journey into wild nature is part of the valuable transition between nature and wild nature; the whole journey is valued and unhurried. Many of the researched benefits on spending time outdoors in an unstructured and unhurried way were identified by practitioners and parents in our survey.

Having time to really BE in nature fosters a love and appreciation of the natural world while reducing stress for the child. Photo taken at Riverside Cottage Nursery.

Alex, the home educator from the Shetland Islands says:

> *The children are calmer. They have the freedom to go outside whenever they want during the day. They can choose, not as they would at school when they can only go outside at certain times. They are able to play freely and develop their imagination without the constraints of a daily school programme. Their learning is more organic, free-range and self-taught, as I feel learning should be.*

Sue, from Boldon Outdoor Nursery listed the following benefits:

> ✿ *Children are healthy and active, with less time away from school with coughs and colds.*
>
> ✿ *They show increased progress in language and communication skills.*
>
> ✿ *They have higher levels of stamina, strength and endurance.*
>
> ✿ *They are able to solve real problems for real reasons.*
>
> ✿ *They are co-constructors of ideas and reason.*
>
> ✿ *They are acquiring a collection of skills that are transferable and will remain with them for life.*
>
> ✿ *They also have lasting memories; children who leave always come back to visit and participate in family events.*

Children are trusted and respected to make good decisions by adults who know them well.

Kimberley, home educator at Day Dreams, reflected on the value of the supportive relationships that develop between children and how this often led to increased engagement with nature:

> *I had two three year olds exploring the garden, one little girl with no shoes on in the mud carrying worms from space to space while a little boy was a little more reserved observing. The little boy at first said 'I don't like mud' but by the end of it he had built a lovely relationship with the little girl and copied her, getting his feet muddy too.*

Exploring in all weathers builds resilience and a sense of community for these children at Nature Nurture who have faced a challenge together.

Terri at Nature Nurture described the benefits of being in wild nature:

> *Children become calmer and increasingly able to self-regulate their emotions. We see increased self and social awareness and empathy. Children become physically fitter and become motivated to be active. Some children have developmental delays and we see a rapid growth in language and communication skills as well as physical and cognitive skills when they have been with us for a few months.*

A staff member of a visiting family centre said:

> *I know that being outdoors is beneficial to children; however they do not often get this opportunity. Being at Nature Nurture allowed me to actually see the benefits and the effects on the children. Children were a lot calmer and able to concentrate because they had had the opportunity for space and freedom to explore the natural world. Children looked physically happier and relaxed by the end of the time they spent at Nature Nurture. The children developed stamina. Importantly, the children became aware of assessing risks for themselves.*

Additional benefits for children with special needs/rights are identified in chapter 3.

Annette from Abacus Filton Hill Preschool commented on the children's increased observational skills and deeper knowledge of nature:

> *Children are more able to express what they see and hear; when they draw and paint they are recalling their experiences in picture form. Their understanding of nature has deepened. They are calmer and they eat more outside and drink water!*

The children themselves commented:

> *'We don't get told off for being muddy; we have fun.'*
>
> *'I like eating in the woods and reading stories.'*
>
> *'I like playing* Goldilocks and the Three Bears *in the woods.'*

Being part of something bigger, working together to create a den through sharing ideas, promotes a sense of community while providing contextual learning in mathematics, engineering, science, technology, literacy and so much more.

Steven at Dunblane Nature Kindergarten also shared the children's views on what they most enjoy at the centre (playing outdoors) with many comments on the wild nature opportunities:

> *'Going outside, to go out to play.'*
>
> *'I like to go out for walks; it's fun to go far.'*
>
> *'Having quiet time around the fire and watching the flames dancing.'*
>
> *'Go for walks in the forest; it can be scary if there is a Gruffalo there.'*
>
> *'Go outside with friends. I like to climb trees and go up high. The fire is good 'cause I cook things to eat.'*
>
> *'Walks, 'cause I see many things, I like birds and their beaks and their wings.'*
>
> *'I like walks 'cause I get to see so many things and I like to see high things and I want to climb up them. I like to see storms, like thunder and lightning. I watched it and feel safe with adults.'*
>
> *'Cooking outside, playing in the sand pit and digging away, then splashing in big muddy bits and getting all mucky.'*
>
> *'I like to play at pretend with my friends when I'm outside.'*

Kim at Orchard Nature Nursery commented on the children's resilience:

> *Risk aware, the children are not scared to try things to test their limits. They are more able to use their imaginations in play situations.*

Kim also shared a comment from a parent valuing childhood as a time to be free to play:

> *What I particularly value is that children can experience the wonderful outdoors which is always accessible and the emphasis on play, letting children be children.*

Luke at Riverside Cottage Nursery identified a broad range of beneficial life skills and well-being factors: 'Overall, confidence, social skills, risk management (reduced accidents), happiness, engagement and so very much more have been experienced and documented by the adults.'

Parents at Riverside Cottage are overall very supportive of the approach and recognise that the children are building memories:

> *They love that their children can experience the things they often did as children.*

Many of the quotes from parents commented on the joyfulness of the experiences:

> *'[The] holistic approach creates an environment where kids can thrive, develop and most of all – have fun.'*
>
> *'They are always tired and happy when I pick them up and often don't want to go home . . . [Riverside Cottage Nursery] provides a very healthy environment that the kids really enjoy.'*
>
> *'Amazing open environment which has brought my daughter on leaps and bounds.'*

Another parent valued the fun children experience at Riverside Cottage:

> *A magical, nature-inspired world of fun, learning and did I mention fun? From roaming with the chickens and splashing in the river, to planting, harvesting and cooking their own food, or maybe building in the workshop, this is education and care like no other . . . an environment where the kids are centre of attention and play trumps process...In this place mud rules OK. And that's just fine by me.*

At Riverside Cottage this young toddler is able to face the world on his own with confidence – and his comforter.

Angela at Alfreton Nursery identified that the nature experiences

> *...encourage resilient children who feel good about themselves and are motivated to learn.*

She also identified emotional well-being, imaginative play, sensory learning, confidence building, having joyful experiences without pressure, breathing in fresh air and a resistance to colds as important benefits.

The journeys are as important as the end point. Children at Nature Nature are not rushed to get to the site but are allowed to investigate what interests them in their own time, nature time.

Public natural spaces enable children to connect with the local community in a natural and uncontrived manner. These children of Into the Woods Outdoor Nursery were delighted to come across workers cutting trees and asked many questions which were patiently answered by the bemused chainsaw users.

Children take some responsibility for the wagon and tools at Nature Nurture, enjoying the challenge, helping and working together to solve problems, building resilience.

Some of the benefits identified by practitioners and parents clearly demonstrate that the benefits of well-being and relationships feature strongly in nature-based play.

In summary, nature-based practice supports the natural joyfulness of childhood. Children are free to play, to be in control, to set the pace, to build meaningful relationships and to just BE. It is an environment where practitioners value, trust, understand and facilitate free play as the way children learn naturally with nature and there is a strong belief in the rights of the child to be consulted in matters that affect them.

> *All children have the right to an education that lays a foundation for the rest of their lives, maximises their ability, and respects their family, cultural and other identities and languages. Children have a right to play and be active participants in all matters affecting their lives.*

United Nations Convention on the Rights of the Child, 1989

Role play happens naturally; here a 'shop' developed in the forest at Nature Nurture; children invited adults to be the clients, creating rules and boundaries that they constantly changed during play. Sensitive adults supported the vulnerable children, enabling them to have control over their play, something that is often lacking in young children's lives.

Learning for sustainability

Emphasis is placed on embedded holistic sustainability by society and the curricula. Sadly, many children have increasingly limited direct contact with nature, instead learning about it through books, nature programmes on television and the internet, often finding this important area very difficult to relate to. Nature-based practice is very closely aligned to sustainable practice and helps children to value and respect the natural environment and community, and naturally leads to responsible citizenship.

According to the report of the One Planet Schools Working Group, all children are entitled to learn about sustainability, and outdoor learning should be a regular feature with progressive curriculum-led experiences:

> *Every learner should have the opportunity for contact with nature in their school grounds on a daily basis and throughout the seasons through the provision of thoughtfully developed green space for outdoor learning and play.*
>
> One Planet School, 2012

According to a report commissioned by Natural England after a two-year pilot study, as many as 10% of children in England have not been to a natural environment in the past year and only 8% of children aged between 6 and 15 visited natural environments with their schools. Interestingly, and not unexpectedly, in households where adults frequently visited natural spaces 82% of the children did so too, while in households where they didn't only 39% of children visited natural spaces frequently (Hunt, Stewart, Burt, and Dillon, 2016).

Nature identity

In order to find out where their place is in nature, children need to develop a nature identity through immersion in the natural world. Close and intimate contact with the natural elements: touching the flowers, feeling the wind, listening to the crickets, tasting the rain, as well as experiences: climbing and hugging trees, sloshing bare feet in the mud, running through the leaves or gently holding a frog, contribute to the building of nature identity. This cannot be learnt from an app or by walking on a path, not touching nature.

> *First, environmental educators need to allow children to be 'untutored savages' for a while. Nature programmes should invite children to make mud pies, climb trees, catch frogs, paint their faces with charcoal, get their hands dirty and their feet wet. They should be allowed to go off the trail and have fun.*
>
> Sobel, *Look, Don't Touch*, 2012

Nature-based practice supports children experiencing contextually and first-hand: life cycles, the water cycle, weather, native species, where food comes from. Through contextual and hands-on opportunities children develop an understanding of their own place in this wonderful natural world.

Nature knowledge and confidence

> *Knowledge without love will not stick. But if love comes first, knowledge is sure to follow.*
>
> Burroughs, John, *Field and Study*, 1919

Human nature is such that we develop a love and a passion for something we are familiar with and have knowledge of, and it is with this passion that the desire comes to protect what we love. Know nature, love nature, protect nature is a logical sequence. Through this increasing knowledge children develop a nature intelligence, intuitively understanding the natural world and their place in it.

A four-year-old child is able to share his understanding of the life cycle of a tree through his illustrations.

An older child at Darvell School is able to share her extensive knowledge about the function and benefits of an oak tree. This interest was gained through regular direct contact with the trees on site.

Knowledge is gained through experience and not through rote learning. A deep understanding of seasonal changes is developed through spending regular periods of time outdoors in all weathers where children will learn about:

- ✿ weather-appropriate clothing
- ✿ how to keep safe in extremes of weather
- ✿ tidal changes along the coast
- ✿ changes in animal behaviour and growth
- ✿ changes in plant growth
- ✿ life cycles.

Where food comes from

Many children no longer experience or know where their food comes from and learning about this is an important part of nature-based practice. Edible berries, seaweed and mushrooms may be collected with the support of experienced gatherers. Herbs, grains, fruit and vegetables can be grown within settings, in a small planter where space is an issue. Children select, plant, water and care for the plants, watching the growth and development before harvesting the produce. At times this may mean that no produce actually ripens, as curious children pull out the carrots to see if they are ready, or that all the produce is eaten before it can be prepared as they graze amongst the strawberries. These opportunities are all part of the science of childhood, exploring and wondering, often leading to further teachable moments.

Preparing the food, being part of the cooking process and ultimately eating the food completes the valuable knowledge and understanding of the food cycle. Peels, stalks and food not eaten can be fed to the animals or composted by the children. Food is never thrown away.

Children of all ages are involved in maintaining and caring for the large organic allotment at Riverside Cottage Nursery, developing an awareness of the full seed-to-plate process.

Luke at Riverside Cottage Nursery reflected on the learning and experiences children have through participating in the day-to-day activities offered through their organic allotment:

> *While this might not at first seem a 'wild space' there are strong connections to be made. Being organic, a huge amount of thought has to go into how the space fits into the local environment and the Scottish weather/temperature/seasons etc. Nature must be understood, for example introducing companion plants used to deter/distract/attract bugs and their natural predators. We must know that it is not natural for one single crop to grow in a large space every single year and that would encourage disease. We must understand that soil health is of huge importance if we aren't going to cram it full of chemicals, and that if we were to use chemicals on our plants what impact that could have on say bees (and of course the devastating knock-on effects of species extinction). This of course extends to building ideas of species extinction, food chains, intricate and complex relationships etc. I could go on, but in summary – growing food brings as strong a connection to and understanding of nature and wild spaces as any other space we visit and is best understood as a part of a broad range of experiences for children at Riverside Cottage Nursery.*

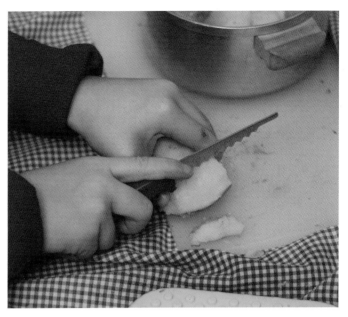

Nature-based practice encourages children to help with food preparation, including using real knives to cut and prepare fruit.

Angela from Alfreton Nursery School shared the development of their edible gardens through community involvement:

> *Parents/carers began to buy trees for the site as leaving presents when their children moved on to 'big school', and this led to fruit trees and different varieties being planted, enhancing our existing native tree collection. As a result of this, these trees now provide snack and ingredients for our regular baking activities, and the children are encouraged to harvest and follow the whole process through to the end, when the peelings are composted as part of our ECO and Healthy School ethos.*

Having real seasonal food in the role play area at Dunblane Nature Kindergarten allows children to explore the smell, feel, weight and even taste of the raw food to gain a deep knowledge of the food they eat as well as the seasonal availability.

HEALTHY EATING

All children, including the babies and toddlers, have easy access to the extensive vegetable gardens at Child First Northampton where they are encouraged to pick their own fresh food. Many will bite straight into the freshly-picked food; this in itself is a rich and worthwhile experience. Tom Shea, the owner, is offered freshly-picked beans by the children.

In the cosy 'family' kitchen, toddlers are mixing dough and making healthy pizzas for lunch.

Children being part of the whole food process is a valuable element of sustainability and is fully supported through nature-based practice. Children develop a knowledge of where food comes from: growing, preparing and eating fresh foods, identifying, picking and eating edible berries and fungi as well as catching their own fish in a stream or in the sea.

On the Shetland Islands where fishing is part of the culture, children have an interest and in-depth knowledge of this industry, knowing where the best places are to fish and what fish to keep for consumption while also having the knowledge to protect the industry by returning undersized fish.

Having a voice – advocacy

Nature-based practice is about children having autonomy, making decisions, taking responsibility and being consulted. These are also the skills needed to become advocates for sustainable practice. Talking, listening, discussing and consulting gives children the tools to voice their views and opinions appropriately. Children's views on nature can be heard and collated in a group project book (see chapter 4) to share with families and raise further awareness of good sustainable practice. Even very young children can be empowered to make changes by reminding others to eat healthily, switch off lights, pick up litter and not waste water.

Respecting culture and place

Children will take ownership of a natural place they have visited regularly and come to love. They will become protective of the natural elements as well as the history of the space and be aware of external damaging influences such as litter and intentional destruction.

Curiosity inspired the children to explore a derelict house on the shoreline on the Shetland Islands. Many questions were asked and photographs taken as they considered what could have caused the damage, as well as wonder at nature that was now growing inside it. This is a space they will revisit over time.

Health and well-being

The health and welfare of the community is important: healthy country, healthy people and healthy people, healthy country. Children having access to healthy fresh food has already been discussed earlier in this chapter.

Children with a high level of well-being are enjoying life, are at ease, spontaneous, self-confident and their mental health is secured. Research has shown that natural environments play a large role in children's well-being.

According to Professor Ferre Laevers, for every child to reach their true potential they need high levels of well-being and high levels of involvement. A child with high levels of well-being is happy, spontaneous and generally enjoying life while an involved child is focused, interested, mentally active and motivated to complete their task to their own satisfaction. For high levels of involvement, opportunities have to offer appropriate challenge.

> *Evidence suggests that the 'involved' child is gaining a deep, motivated, intense and long-term learning experience.*
>
> Csikszentmihayli 1979; Laevers 1994

It's easy to see the effect when you watch children play outside. Children are different when they're outdoors; free of school pressures and harried schedules, they relax and simply become children. In fact, according to one study, children's stress levels fall within minutes of seeing green spaces, making outside play a simple, no-cost and time efficient antidote for an overstressed child. (Kuo, 2004)

Testing the flexibility of this branch allows the child at Riverside Cottage Nursery to develop a knowledge of the strength of such thinner branches. Occasionally a branch might break but through this, children increase their knowledge and respect of nature.

Impacting on nature

Anything and everything we do in nature has an impact on nature. Some impacts may be positive, others less so. It is the degree of impact and the necessity of that impact that needs to be considered. Animals use the natural environment for dens, nests and play. Humans are part of nature and are also 'animals' and part of this ecosystem. It is about finding a balance between the impact children's play may have and the long-term benefits to both children and the natural environment of such direct exposure to nature.

Play in wild nature will have an environmental impact. Supporting young children in recognising and identifying such impact, empowers them to act responsibly now and in the future as they experience and consider:

✿ compaction of pathways through overuse, thereby increasing the density of the soil

✿ destruction of native plant species

✿ destruction of animal habitats

✿ denudation of natural spaces through the overuse of resources, for example using up all the available sticks as firewood.

> *For special places to work their magic on kids they need to be able to do some clamber and damage. They need to be free to climb trees, muck about, catch things, and get wet— above all, to leave the trail.*
>
> Pyle, 2002

Look but don't touch?

> *Children's emotional and affective values of nature develop earlier than their abstract, logical and rational perspectives.*
>
> Kellert, 2002

Children use all their senses as they investigate and make sense of the world around them. Tactile or kinaesthetic children in particular need to 'feel' nature. A common-sense approach is required, weighing up the benefits of children immersed in nature, gaining knowledge and a connection to nature, as opposed to the long-term risks to both nature and the child of not developing this connection. By encouraging an enhanced connecting, a sense of belonging and identity in the natural environment and being part of something much bigger, is realised.

Through exploring water, soil and mud within the garden at Dunblane Nature Kindergarten, children develop a contextual knowledge of the impact their play has on the space which they can then transfer to natural spaces beyond the gate.

DEVELOPING EMPATHY

A seven-year-old boy on the Shetland Islands found a small hedgehog while walking, and worried: 'He is going in the road. The cars could kill him'. He tried redirecting it gently but the hedgehog seemed determined to walk into the road. After some consideration he gently picked it up and moved it to a safer spot. A hedgehog was later spotted on the other side of the road and he 'knew' it was his hedgehog and that it had safely crossed the road. This was a moment of great empathy and care for this living creature, some might say he should not have touched it but celebrating his concern for the hedgehog was at that stage of greater importance.

David Sobel has stated that children aged between the ages of 6 and 12 have an innate desire to explore forests, to dig and build dens. I believe that this is also evident in much younger children. These activities are natural ways for children to develop environmental values. Every time we stop children from touching or having direct contact with nature we stop them from naturally learning and teach them that nature is boring and often dangerous.

It is the adult's role to foster children's capacity to understand and respect the natural world and to realise the interdependence between the land, the plants and the animals. It is these stewardship values that will make children advocates for the natural environment as they grow up.

> *Could it be that our fear of litigation and our puritanical concerns for protecting each and every blade of grass are hampering the development of the very stewardship values and behaviors that we environmental educators all say we're trying to foster? I believe so.*

Sobel, 2012

Collecting natural resources

Children develop a fascination for natural objects that they have found and naturally want to keep these to take back to show parents, teachers and other children. They will proudly tell detailed stories and facts about their treasures and often these are kept and carried around for a long time.

A handful of carefully-selected autumn leaves collected and carried around the site become a treasure for this child at Nature Nurture. Weighing up the long-term harm and benefits to this child and to the environment is given equal weight on deciding if natural resources should be removed from the site.

How do we deal with children wanting to keep sticks or shells? Consider the environmental impact of removing a few selected shells from the public beach to the impact of adults walking or vehicles driving on beaches. Buying shells without knowing if they come from a licensed dealer and are sustainably sourced could be more environmentally harmful. Reflect and decide what you are comfortable with. My personal view is to borrow and then return nature to nature when children have finished exploring instead of gluing it down or throwing it in the bin. Other considerations:

❀ Agree a limit to the numbers collected and return them to nature later.

❀ Remove three pieces of litter or alien species/weeds in exchange for accessing the site.

❀ Create photo ID charts to help children identify unwanted plants and clear sections of their wild space of alien vegetation.

Such strategies are positive and model good sustainable practice.

Places, where children's stress levels are reduced and where things are constantly changing sustains children's curiosity and involvement. Wild nature *is* the perfect natural learning environment – it does not need to be created, it has already been created by nature itself, and it is perfect.

NBP in action

SHARING FOUND TREASURES

In Australia, Jenelle Haskew, created small treasure books with envelopes for children to collect their treasures in: a feather, a seedpod, a flower or a red leaf to fit in an envelope. This encouraged children to select only one or two small 'treasures'.

At the centre, children transfer their treasures into small origami boxes made of recycled paper to create a community display that can be revisited. They started bringing in and sharing treasures from their homes, connecting centre and community.

Sharing found treasures with the community.

Chapter 3

Shaping your vision

Now you've read about the benefits of nature-based practice and decided you want to implement something similar into your setting, it is time to shape the vision for your individual provision.

Having and holding on to a vision

It is important to have a vision as an individual and as a team. Without a clear vision the way ahead can become unclear, particularly during times of challenge. Visions can and should change as experiences influence new thinking.

All the practitioners interviewed for this book had a clear vision (each is detailed on the case study pages). Their visions included wanting to take children into local wild spaces, encouraging them to play and develop a sense of belonging to the space. They wanted them to develop a love and respect for their environment. At times practitioners may be tempted to bring the wild space back to the classroom but the wild spaces *are* the classroom and the outdoors *is* the learning place. Wild nature is the best learning environment and needs no changing or setting up.

A clear vision will become the vision of the community.

The rest of this chapter covers key areas to consider when developing your vision. Before reading them, think back to chapter 1 and the current models of nature-based practice. What is going to work for you?

As previously mentioned we are all on a journey. Here are some points to reflect on.

How often would you like to take children out into wild nature?

- Occasional outings away from the setting, maybe annually or quarterly.
- Weekly outings lasting two to three hours, for a block of six or eight weeks.
- Weekly or twice-weekly outings, for half a day or a full day, throughout the year.
- Daily access for shorter periods of time, possibly because you have a suitable space within the playground.
- Every day for prolonged periods of time throughout the year.

In addition have you considered these variations?

- The numbers and ages of the children you would take out with you.
- How far you would allow children to roam freely.
- The opportunities the children will have access to and possible activities you would offer.
- The amount of adult involvement, including the freedom, directions or instructions you would give the children.
- The type of resources or equipment you would make available to the children.

The role of the adult

> *Learning and teaching should not stand on opposite banks and just watch the river flow by; instead, they should embark together on a journey down the water. Through an active, reciprocal exchange, teaching can strengthen learning and how to learn.*
>
> Malaguzzi, 1998

Adult supervision in childcare environments is mandatory and children will not be able to enjoy the total freedom that comes with being in an adult-free space. However, creating 'adult interference free' spaces offers children the perception of freedom so sadly lacking in many children's lives. By stepping back, preferably sitting down, adults facilitate working with the natural flow and rhythm found in nature, being 'with' the child in *their* natural time. Adults become an ally to learning.

The role of practitioners in nature-based practice is crucial. By being mindful and attentive around children, practitioners will observe individual play behaviours and play cues, getting to really know and understand each child and their thinking. In order to become a skilled nature pedagogue there are a number of key objectives to consider and put into practice.

Children and practitioner on a journey together, the adult mindful and sensitive to the needs of the children at Boldon Nursery School, Outdoor Nursery.

Remembering childhood

Practitioners observing children in wild nature often reflect on their own childhood with great fondness. They reminisce about time spent exploring freely, building dens, climbing trees and building dams in the rivers. These are valuable memories and emotions, so hold onto them and use them to advocate for children's rights to create similar memories. Childhood is a time to make memories. Wouldn't it be sad if our children didn't have fond childhood memories of the outdoors to share with their own children and grandchildren?

Become a reflective action researcher

Action researchers explore methodologies, make changes, reflect and analyse such changes. Just because something has been done a certain way for 20 years does not mean it needs to be done that way for the next 20 years. Nature pedagogues are action researchers, they are reflective in their practice, they are brave, they have the courage and the risk-taking disposition to try new ways of approaching practice.

Kirsty Liljegren in Australia recognises that their practice at Cornish College ELC has changed as their understanding of what is important to children, what matters and how they learn continues to develop. She expresses gratitude to the philosophy from Reggio Emilia:

> *... which has taught us to listen deeply, with all our senses to what is happening with children, and to research, to be learners ourselves about children and learning ...'*

Through asking questions, reflecting and exploring options, our thinking can continuously be challenged and reviewed, and your vision for the setting can be defined and continually adapted. Some of the reflective questions Kirsty and her team shared were:

> ♦ *What does nature mean for children?*
>
> ♦ *What actually is it that we seem to be witnessing? It is hard to put into words, but the emotion is evident as we observe and engage with children in the great outdoors.*
>
> ♦ *How do families perceive this experience?*
>
> ♦ *How will this inform/change our programme back at the centre?*
>
> ♦ *What matters to the children in this place?*
>
> ♦ *How will this inform our practice?*

'Does nature mean the same to everyone?' was an investigation undertaken by Kirsty and the children.

Different questions arose over time as their community researched together. It is such ongoing, critical and receptive reflection that ensures continuous high-quality experiences.

Here are some more reflective questions to consider as you start to shape your vision.

❀ What are your favourite childhood memories?

❀ Why do you think these memories are so powerful?

❀ How can you provide opportunities for children in your care to have the same memories?

❀ What outdoor opportunities would you like to offer the children in your care?

❀ Do you feel comfortable with allowing children to take risks?

❀ How do you feel about being in nature?

❀ Why do you want to take children into wild nature?

PARENTAL REFLECTION

Goodstart Red Hill in Australia offers a 'Nature in the City' programme where parental views are valued. Susannah McKelvey is a speech pathologist and parent of a three-year-old:

> 'Ben tells us more about what he and his peers and teachers do on nature walks than any of the rest of his time spent in daycare. Some of the things that Ben has told us spontaneously are:
>
> "I threw rocks in the water."
>
> "I found a wriggly worm."
>
> "I didn't go in the water; I just sat and watched."
>
> "Look at your big shadow. It's like mine on my nature walk."
>
> "I picked up some pretty leaves."
>
> It is wonderful that he is observing and actively engaged in these activities and lovely for us that he shares his experiences. He also loves bringing home 'souvenirs', which are as precious to him as a painting or clay sculpture he has created. We have had lots of special sticks and a ceramic tile, which he drew around back at the centre. Unfortunately it was dropped and broken at home, but now it's a jigsaw.'

Such community feedback is valuable and should be considered in the reflective process of the centre.

Further reflective questions you could ask to improve your practice in different areas are listed below.

Learning and teaching

✿ Do we need to be present for children to learn?

✿ Do we always need to teach, to ask questions, to tell or show children what to do?

✿ Could being a silent practitioner allow children the freedom to fully engage with the environment and their own learning?

Routines and structure

✿ For whose benefit are the current routines and structure in place? Are these flexible to cater for individual needs?

✿ Do we have an agenda that interferes with the children's needs?

✿ Do we allow for children's natural flow and rhythm?

When children are interested and curious they will lead their own learning.

Risk and safety

✿ Do we appreciate that we are responsible for both the emotional and the physical well-being of the children in our care?

✿ Do we see children are capable and competent, that they do not go out to intentionally harm themselves?

✿ Could we look at finding the balance between our own anxieties and the children's desire to be adventurous?

Behaviour

✿ Is a large proportion of our time spent monitoring behaviour?

✿ Could it be that we have unrealistic expectations of children?

✿ What would happen if there were minimal rules?

Photo: Jenelle Haskew

To enable minimal disruption to children's play, tired children sleep outdoors in hammocks.

Practice trust and respect

We refer to some over-protective parents as 'helicopter parents'. In the same way, 'helicopter practitioners' hover around children, patrolling, constantly monitoring behaviour, safety, learning, routines and time. However, in nature-based practice, children are trusted, agreements are reached and there are minimal adult rules to be enforced. 'Supervisors' are not required.

Practitioner 'interference free' space

The practitioner's role is to support and facilitate the involvement and well-being of the children. When children are involved, the adult's role is to be mindful, aware, alert and not to alter the child's state of 'flow' by needlessly interrupting.

There is a fine line between interaction and interference. Being able to judge when and at what level to enter children's play is a skill developed through practice. To get it right, adults working with children need to be skilled observers and sensitive responders as children engage with the environment. This can be difficult when the adults are hovering, when there is an adult perception that there are other things that need to be done, or when routines and structure take priority over the children's play.

Adults sensitively enter children's play to stimulate their interest or further their knowledge. At times this interaction may be immediate, while at other times further investigation should be undertaken when children have finished playing. This little girl is discovering that the fresh sea lettuce is edible. 'Salty and sandy' was her verdict.

NBP in action

RIPPING UP THE RULE BOOK

What would happen if there were minimum rules? Many adult rules don't make sense to the children, which is why they may need constant monitoring and reinforcing. In a university study, Swanson School in New Zealand abandoned the playground rules completely, much to the reported horror of some teachers at the time. Principal Bruce McLachlan commented:

'Mudslides, skateboarding, and tree climbing kept the children so occupied the school no longer needed a timeout area or as many teachers on patrol. The school is actually seeing a drop in bullying, serious injuries and vandalism, while concentration levels in class are increasing. The kids were motivated, busy and engaged. In my experience, the time children get into trouble is when they are not busy, motivated and engaged. It's during that time they bully other kids, graffiti or wreck things around the school.' (Study by AUT and Otago University)

Interestingly, with fewer teachers 'on patrol' there was an increase in risky play but a reduction in serious injuries and bullying. Also of interest is that the children's concentration levels inside the classroom increased. These are similar findings to those experienced in nature-based practice.

Children do not need adult-enforced rules to self-risk assess – in fact these reduce children's capabilities as they stop thinking for themselves.

Children, like adults, at times need to just *be* and not to have adults concerned about them doing 'nothing' or being bored, and therefore filling their time. In nature-based practice, practitioners are aware of children's natural play; they are sensitive responders and skilled observers.

Adults can be fully engaged, fully there for children, without hands-on involvement or, as so often happens, taking over their play. Children as the decision-makers are quite capable of following their own interests when the natural environment offers so much variety and choice.

Responsive and insightful observers

Skilled nature-pedagogues are:

✿ **Silent** (more often than not). They focus on listening rather than talking, value and do not interrupt the natural flow of play, and don't raise their voices unless there is an emergency.

✿ **Responsive**. They respectfully enter play to enrich learning rather than offer instruction.

✿ **Insightful**. They engage in meaningful observations, identify the learning taking place, reflect, analyse and plan further scaffolding extensions.

✿ **Adaptable**. They are flexible and follow the children's interest.

✿ **Relaxed**. They are calm and tuned into the children and the environment.

What does this mean in practice? Find a comfortable non-intrusive place to sit and observe the group. Be fully mindful: listen, watch, observe body language and sensitively step in when required or requested by the children. Record, reflect, analyse, assess and plan as appropriate to the benefit of children and families.

Teaching skills

Nature-based practice is a community of learning and teaching. Some knowledge and skills – those that will allow children to develop, to become independent and to keep as safe as necessary – are actively taught. These might include:

✿ the use of books or computers to increase knowledge

✿ the function and appropriate use of tools and equipment

✿ functional skills such as basket weaving and tying knots

✿ information about hidden hazards to develop self-risk assessing skills.

Information can be presented in many different ways that can inspire and encourage a love of learning. Think of it as a gift and allow children to do their own unwrapping. Nature-based practice is exciting, the young investigators do their own exploring and discovering and, if we are lucky, they share this with us.

The practitioner supports a child's interest in a colourful feather found, modelling how to research for the right bird in a pictorial reference book.

At times it may be helpful to ask a critical friend to observe the ethos and adult interaction with the children. Juliet Robertson reflected on her experience after visiting Dunblane Nature Kindergarten:

> " *The interactions of the staff with the children were a pleasure to witness outside and in. They were all calm and gentle with the children. There were no raised voices and adults' talking did not dominate - gentle laughter and encouragement was heard. When I asked the staff about this, they told me, 'We videoed each other to observe our interactions – being patient, pausing after a child has spoken, not interrupting and whether we get down to child-height when we interact. We have learned about how to get a good overview space in every classroom and in the outdoor space.'* "

The practitioner has settled in a place where she has an overview of the children at play. She is fully there and mindful of what is happening should the children need her or she feels she needs to step in.

Supporting children with additional needs

All children have rights, and children with additional needs have special rights. All children have the right to 'belong' and, where practically possible, no obvious distinction is made between children of different capabilities. Every child is unique, and adults try to put in place appropriate support so that where possible, all children have the same high-quality experiences, which includes experiences in nature. The provision you can provide for all children in your care should be considered when you are defining your vision.

Angela Green from Child First says that:

> The main benefits which we have observed have been for our children with additional needs (such as global delay and autism) who attend the setting. These children have been exposed to the same experiences and have not been restricted by their conditions. They are encouraged and included and have thrived from being offered the opportunity to access the outdoors and woodland. The children with language delay benefit from the smaller group sizes when participating in Forest School sessions and by the end of the six-week programme have found a voice and their place within the group, having the confidence to express themselves and talk about their needs and experiences.

NBP in action

BENEFITS IDENTIFIED IN THE NATURE/NURTURE EARLY INTERVENTION PROGRAMMES

Speaking to parents, children, teachers and specialists about this programme has identified a number of important benefits for the children involved.

At a core group meeting on the 8th December, the school reported a dramatic turnaround in J's behaviour:

'She has been working well in class, appearing happier, improved social skills and showing a sense of humour. J is also taking part in the school pantomime, which she had refused to do in the past. There have been some instances where J has become upset but it has been resolved more quickly than previously. J seems more confident and is able to make and keep friends and seems more open, she has been able to speak to me more, although it seems she can still be guarded. It is felt that the Nature Nurture group has been able to help J in so many ways. There has been such a positive change in J.'
(Headteacher)

'A 'Looked After Children's Review', held in October, has formally acknowledged how influential the project has been in supporting T to increase his self awareness, his coping strategies and skill base. In particular, there has been a marked improvement in his social interaction skills. T's foster carers have told me that they have seen more positive progress over the time of Nature Nurture Project than in the five years he has been placed with them.'
(Social worker)

'As you know, everyone has been delighted with the progress T has made whilst attending Nature Nurture sessions. T himself describes the past 12 months as the "best of his life so far" and his care network have seen huge developments in his social, relationship and empathy skills. Nature Nurture has played a leading role in taking this forward after years of limited progress in these areas.'
(Social worker)

'Thank you very much to all the staff as C is much more confident with walking and it has helped her in becoming a well-rounded individual, and more sociable with others, especially adults, whom she used to shy away from. Well done all!'
(Parent)

'My hope is that funding is made available to allow the project to continue running, as my first hand knowledge and experience has allowed me to witness the positive change that can be achieved in a young person's life in a relatively short period of time.'
(Staff member, Craigielea Children's Centre)

'I've lost weight. I don't lose my cool any more; Nature Nurture has helped me become more mature.'
(Richard, 12)

'This has been the best time of my life. I wish I could keep coming forever!'
(Greg, 13)

'I really like seeing everyone each week. We've made a club and I got to be leader. I fell out with one of the boys but I was really happy 'cause I managed to sort it out and now we are friends again.'
(Aidan, 10)

'I wish we could do a sponsored walk or something to get the money you need to run Nature Nurture forever. I want to come back in after Christmas and in the summer too. It helps me such a lot by coming here!'
(Levi, 11)

Additional physical support

Children with mobility limitations often have the same desire to experience risk, to go fast, to go high, to lie in the cool grass or feel the warm beach sand.

A challenge for all may be facilitating those who need mobility aids: it is not easy to negotiate an uneven forest track or soft sand. Investing in an all-terrain vehicle with inflatable wheels or a trolley with large soft wheels could be a solution and allow a different experience. Asking the children, finding out what they would like to do, and thinking how we can make it happen often pushes adults to try innovative ways of doing things differently.

All children need access to exciting natural opportunities. Collecting their own autumn leaves and threading them on a twig is a motivational and sensorial activity benefitting fine motor development and well-being. This might mean adults having to reflect on how to provide such experiences if children lack mobility.

Challenging behaviours

From my experience, there are very few behavioural issues when children are out in a natural environment. There are so many opportunities to challenge themselves, to follow their interests and with a reduction in adult restrictions and structure and an increase in trust, children tend to have high levels of well-being and don't feel the need to push or challenge the adults.

Practitioners' fears that children might not follow agreements or run away from the group could require increased adult-child ratios according to their benefit-risk assessments until educators and children feel comfortable in the space.

Autism and other disorders

Many children on the autism spectrum or with ADD, or ADHD thrive in natural environments. This is where they feel they have freedom, where things are calmer, enabling them to focus and to engage as well as having 'permission' to be louder, not constantly being reminded to use 'inside voices'.

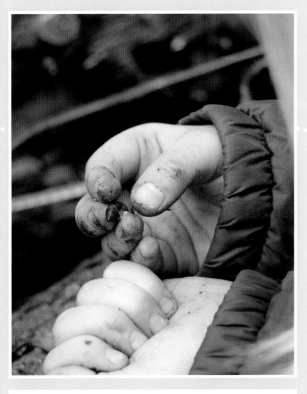

Children's natural learning disposition through nature is supported by sensorial hands-on experiences for all children. This child is carefully investigating a tiny pupa found in the grass whilst being supported to be on the damp ground.

'I liked everything we did.'
(Jodie, 11)

'I wish I could be here forever.'
(Jordan, 9)

'I like riding the donkeys and going on the rope swing and helping to light the fire.'
(Jenna, 9)

'I liked picking apples and pressing them and making apple juice.'
(Courtney, 11)

A young boy I worked with who has Asperger's syndrome initially took time away from the group in the forest, walking to a nearby clearing and pacing for a few minutes before re-joining the group. As the week progressed, he took less time out until he no longer felt the need to move away, and started participating in and even leading imaginative play.

Finding a place to just be, to quietly reflect and observe, is therapeutic and calming in what is often a hectic and overstimulating artificial world. Appropriate clothing and support for children with mobility issues are vital here.

Listening to parental concerns

By including families and the community in the planning and development of a programme possible obstacles that might appear later can be avoided. (See chapter 4 for more on involving all stakeholders).

In all of the interviews conducted for this book, practitioners talked about how they gave families and the community the opportunity to express their views, and not surprisingly there were a number of common concerns. Each situation is different, but the important thing is to listen and acknowledge that the parent has a right to their opinion.

Families need to be aware of the philosophy and ethos of practice when they first express an interest in your setting. In this way you may be able to allay the concerns of some parents.

Steven at Dunblane Nature Kindergarten had a nature vision for the centre which differed from the practice at the time:

> *'At the start of the project, prior to being employed, I held a family consultation to share the vision. Parents were concerned that I would close down the indoor setting, and about where the children would consume food, how the children would learn, where they would go to the toilet and how we would manage being out in all weathers.' Steven addressed these concerns: 'I replied during the session, in a calm and detailed manner how we would support children and how in my belief this approach would provide a rounded full body ethos to children learning and attaining knowledge.'*

Kimberley from Day Dreams talked about explaining the setting's approach to parents:

> *When parents initially come for a tour I explain in depth the importance of outdoor play. If it is not for them, they know from the start. I explain the importance for children's holistic development, show photos of the children's beaming faces, and that usually puts them at ease.*

Luke (from Riverside Cottage Nursery):

> *We are very straightforward now in saying that we cannot change our belief and approach based on one family's dislike of a particular part of our practice. This is of course done in a friendly way; and we tell parents that choice is a great thing and we simply aren't the place for everybody.*

The parents at Annette (Filton Hill Preschool) and Kim's (Orchard Nature Nursery) settings were concerned about practicalities:

> *'Mud'* is what Kim said parents were concerned about! She solved this by making *'waterproof suits available and ensuring parents are warned that children get muddy!'*

Similarly, Annette said:

> *Some expressed initial worries about clothes getting dirty, so we discussed the use of old clothes and the benefits for their children.*

Sharing the journey with families at Dunblane Nature Kindergarten enabled parents to be active participants with a trust and belief in even their two-year-olds accessing natural spaces such as the river.

Photo: Sue Stokoe

Children do not get sick from being in the cold; this was one of the misconceptions Boldon School Nursery addressed with the parents.

Sue from Boldon Outdoor Nursery shared some of the parental concerns she had experienced:

> ◆ *Children being out in the cold – the misconception that this leads to illness.*
>
> ◆ *How do they learn to read and write when they are outside?*
>
> ◆ *They are dirty all of the time.*
>
> ◆ *Transition into school.*

Sue addresses these concerns in a number of ways including practical support for families concerned about clothing and muddy children:

> ◆ *Sharing our ethos during home visits before a child starts nursery and consistently across the year.*
>
> ◆ *Utilising the power of parents, from one parent to another. Current parents host meetings and gatherings for new parents, spreading the word, sharing the concept and answering the questions, which they do magnificently!*
>
> ◆ *Constantly inviting parents into the school to work alongside and develop an understanding of the powerful learning outdoors has upon their child.*
>
> ◆ *Gathering feedback at every event/workshop/day where relevant.*
>
> ◆ *Changing the standard uniform to a kit, moving away from the school skirt and trousers to layers of warm clothing being the most important.*
>
> ◆ *Providing a wet room (shower), lots of spare clothes and toiletries should parents wish to use them. (If going straight out after nursery, they may need to clean up their child.)*

Did you know you need to develop 50 muscles in your body before you can even hold a pen to write?

The children are taught new skills such as using wire cutters, peelers and snips. These tools are developing strength in the muscles in your child's hands – the small ones that will help your child to hold a pen or pencil and use it with control.

Parents, as the primary caregiver, want what is best for their child. Effective mentoring and support will help parents understand the philosophy of the centre and how this will benefit their child. Poster created by Boldon Nursery Outdoor Nursery.

The benefits of potentially risky play and opportunities are shared with parents. Making parents aware of procedures and practice can be shared through photographs. This little boy at Riverside Cottage is waving goodbye to the practitioners to let them know that he is moving away. Adults keep in contact with walkie talkies and can alert another practitioner that he is on his way.

Concerns about risk

It is important that you acknowledge the parents' desire for their children to be safe, and reassure them about the children's growing knowledge in keeping themselves safe. Practitioners can share their benefit-risk assessments (there is more in chapter 5 about this) and talk to parents about the issues that might emerge if children are overly protected. With this information parents can make an informed decision.

Some of the concerns Angela Green's parents at Child First had were:

> *The children will hurt themselves, they are not capable, the area is not secure, stranger danger. We down-play any concerns and explain the benefits that accessing outdoors brings to the children. We reassure parents that instead of having more injuries, we actually have less injuries as having the ability to explore and risk take makes children better (able to keep themselves safe).*

Luke shared that at Riverside Cottage Nursery:

> *In the past, parents have expressed many concerns around safety, children wandering away (there is little to physically stop children leaving the premises if they wish to) and more. The main concern parents have is around the river we use – expecting children to float away to the sea or something along those lines.*

Luke has addressed these concerns with:

> *Loads of parent information about the setting and our practice – also sharing articles and encouraging parents to seek out and share articles. Bringing parents in regularly to experience what we do and understand the ideas behind it has also been helpful. Essentially, not just aiming for parents to accept our approach but positively advocate and wholeheartedly believe in it.*

Concerns about weather

Some parents are worried about the weather, so practitioners provided the families with information about appropriate clothing and footwear. Some parents may be concerned that their children will catch a cold or become ill when it is cold and wet and request that they are kept indoors. This is where the practitioner confidently needs to share their knowledge that the cold does not cause infections; germs spread through close contact, often in warm indoor spaces which act as incubators for the multiplication of germs. Settings that value outdoor play should have a no-cancellation policy on outdoor play.

Luke shares his experience from Riverside Cottage Nursery:

> *We used to experience families turning up in the morning and telling staff that their child can't go outside today as they have a cold or they are in some way ill. When it comes to children having colds, it has been an uphill struggle trying to promote the idea that bacteria don't live out in the snow. We now (rightly or wrongly) simply say that if your child is too sick to go out, they are too sick to attend Riverside, as we are an outdoor nursery.*

Concerns about hygiene

Some parents may express concerns about mud, washing hands and general hygiene outdoors. Parental concerns should be seen as possibilities to change practice – more often than not it becomes an opportunity, perhaps for practitioners to improve their own practice.

The weather and the environment become irrelevant when children and adults are wearing appropriate clothing at Dunblane Nature Kindergarten.

Sitting around the fire on a cold, wet day eating a steaming cup of healthy soup brings children and adults together as they share in this 'ritual' at Secret Garden Nursery.

Fresh water and hot drinks are available for the children at Boldon Nursery School, Outdoor Nursery. They freely access the wooden hut, helping themselves to these to cool down or warm up.

Concerns about curriculum learning and development

Children in outdoor environments benefit developmentally as evidenced by numerous research projects. Luke made the observation at Riverside Cottage Nursery that providing for the child's interest …

> is the most appropriate thing developmentally for any particular child at any given time. It seems the children know more about how they grow, develop and learn than adults.

Some parents may express their concern about the lack of what they perceive to be 'proper' academics – concerns that the required curriculum may not be covered through their perception that outdoor learning is not 'proper' schooling. Alex as a home-school parent on the Shetland Islands has no such concerns and has had visits from the local education authority home link teacher which have all been satisfactory with no issues.

This concern about what children are doing and learning is a valid one for parents, and can be addressed through documentation (see chapter 4) making the learning visible and holding regular parent information meetings where the practitioners share the learning that's taking place.

Planning for Opportunities and Possibilities

Learning opportunities
FOCUS Understanding the World
The World
Change and growth
Understanding the seasonal changes and what affect this has upon the allotment
Research /referencing to find out information
Links to home- growing own produce, allotments at home.
Understanding of life cycles
Exploring life and death of crops
Caring for and nurturing livestock and crops; Feeding, watering and weeding the raised beds, checking for eggs and changing bedding for chickens.
Language development – new vocabulary, sharing thoughts, communicating with others
Revisiting and recalling through consistent care routines
Understanding the origins of food
Social experiences, children will share their own experiences of allotments and gardens.

Role of the Adult
Taking responsibility for the children's understanding of how to care for all areas of the allotment as this may be a unique opportunity for many children.

ALLOTMENT

LIVESTOCK   RAISED BEDS

POTTING SHED

Involve children and parents in developing, maintaining and resourcing the area.

Possibilities
Scientific enquiry
Introducing children to different research materials to develop their understanding of different crops.
Children see the entire cycle of a plant; Planting, developing, producing food, preparing to cook, eating.
Look at sharing the food which they have harvested to develop children's relationships with others and their meals.
Understanding time. Children will see how long it takes for plants to grow and develop. Look at ideas of how to track and record development and support the children's memories over the course of the whole process.

Children can research what types of plants grow in different climates and what would be best to plant and when. Offer different types of vegetation for different seasons e.g.. Flowers, herbs, foods.

Communication and Language
Development of new vocabulary
Mathematical development
measuring, recording change/growth/size

Boldon Nursery School, Outdoor Nursery displays laminated information on the learning opportunities available through various experiences throughout the setting.

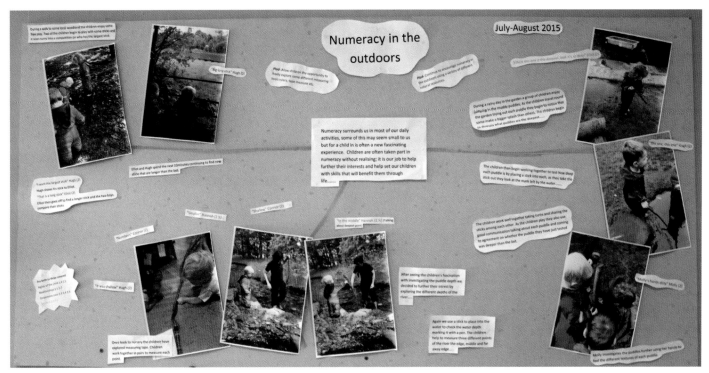

Documentation on this parent information board at Dunblane Nature Kindergarten shares the contextual numeracy children have access to outdoors.

Advice and tips from practitioners

Each practitioner has their own personal message to give to others contemplating excursions into wild nature. These messages come from the valuable personal experiences developed as part of each individual's journey into wild nature.

Steven's advice (Dunblane Nature Kindergarten):

"
- ◆ *Always have a camera or other method to capture the moment.*

- ◆ *Check the weather report prior to embarking on your journey, and be prepared for it to change at short notice.*

- ◆ *Ensure you have a method of contact (mobile phone, walkie talkie – dependent on range strength), and all emergency contact details (laminated).*

- ◆ *If possible, familiarise yourself with the environment prior to exploring it with children, gauge the fauna and flora of the area. If you are unable to visit then adopt a common sense approach and assess the environment with the group.*

- ◆ *Create a benefit-risk assessment with the children.*

- ◆ *Children and adults should be dressed appropriately for the environment they are in, or going to.*

- ◆ *Always have a first aid kit available (tailored for outdoors).*

- ◆ *Take extra food, water, spare clothing (minimum to carry) and an emergency shelter (bivi).*

- ◆ *Have a plan B and then a plan C for your time outdoors, then prepare yourself to follow no plan at all; the real plan should be to follow the plan that the children allow you to follow.*
"

Kim's advice (Orchard Nature Nursery):

"
- ◆ *Don't plan! Take resources which allow free flow child-led activities to happen.*

- ◆ *Allow the children to take risks – they know what they can and cannot do – be there only as support and knowledge if required.*
"

Terri's adivce (Nature Nurture):

"
- ◆ *Create clear routines and structures that are flexible and responsive to the children's needs and interests.*

- ◆ *Conduct benefit-risk analysis rather than risk assessments. Ensure you know what the benefits are to being in a location or following an activity first, and then ensure that this is balanced against the hazards and potential risks.*

- ◆ *Allow enough time for free play and revisit locations or activities regularly over a period of time to allow for repetition and deep engagement.*

- ◆ *Focus on enabling rather than restricting and on strengths rather than weaknesses.*

- ◆ *Allow time, space and continuity for relationships to flourish.*
"

Alex's advice (a home educator on the Shetland Islands):

"
- ◆ *As an adult be there as a guide. Do not see yourself as a teacher or instructor. Allow the children to be taught by wild nature. Obviously when lighting fires, cooking etc. simple instructions and guidance will have to be given especially with young children. It always surprises me how versatile and imaginative children are in nature and the amazing inventions and ways of being and playing they develop when left unprompted by adults.*

- ◆ *Travel light. You don't need to carry toys, seats, man-made materials with you. Obviously you may need some food and water but be inventive, make the most of all the natural resources nature has to offer. Build a shelter from branches, cook your food over a fire. Drink your water from a natural source or boil some to drink. Make nature art and decorate your landscape with your creations so that others visiting the area will be inspired.*

- ◆ *Allow the children to run free, to create their own boundaries. This is one of the most important areas of a child's development because when they can set their own boundaries – they learn their own limitations as well as their abilities. There are far too many instances of adults imposing boundaries on children from preschool age through school age and then into adulthood where we still encounter restrictions.*

- ◆ *To me, the most important point to remember is that children are naturally connected and tuned into our natural world in a far greater way than we are as adults. This is due mainly to the fact that our culture does not encourage us as adults to nurture and maintain our innocent, child-like awe and wonder of the world as we did when we were children. Don't hinder children's natural wild, playful instincts. Don't block their wonderful curiosity and natural learning. Let them be free so that they grow into secure, well-rounded, self-sustaining adults who pass on their love of nature to the next generation.*
"

Kimberley's advice (Day Dreams):

> *Let the children be free and be led by them. You are their role model so get excited and not scared around them; really embrace it because it is crucial for their development.*

Angela Green's advice (Child First):

> *Just do it, you will be surprised at their ability and confidence. Trust them...*

Sue's advice (Boldon Outdoor Nursery):

> ♦ *The pedagogical journey of the team, together, is vital when leading and implementing any change. This has to be carefully thought through, planned and have quality time allocated to it.*
>
> ♦ *Adults must be confident, committed and motivated.*
>
> ♦ *Talk with the children and parents; acknowledge any fears they may have.*
>
> ♦ *Be aware of the need to carry out a dynamic risk assessment in relation to the weather on the day.*
>
> ♦ *Don't over organise, don't take control.*
>
> ♦ *Time outside should not be about having a set of planned outcomes/products you want the children to achieve/make.*
>
> ♦ *Ensure appropriate clothing for adults and children.*
>
> ♦ *Be prepared to give children time and space (things take a lot longer in nature).*

Taking a risk – doing it 'my' way. Practitioners at Boldon Outdoor Nursery use written benefit risk assessments as well as doing dynamic risk assessments on the weather, rain means the stile will be slippery.

Luke's advice (Riverside Cottage):

> ♦ *Building strong bonds and trusting relationships with children is the absolute key to enjoying wild nature. When mutual trust exists, children use adults as a support to facilitate their exploration and know the adult isn't there to ruin their play or exert power over their experiences. This makes children far more likely to seek help and guidance if needed rather than sneaking off to do something away from adult support.*
>
> ♦ *Allowing children to get hurt, experiencing pain and fear is a part of this. This encourages children to assess the risk around them for themselves and their peers as they don't assume an adult will step in before anything unwanted happens. They should know that an adult's advice, care, love and concern is genuine so that on those (what become very rare) occasions where a child's experience doesn't allow for them to see the dangers of a situation, they will trust the adult warning them.*
>
> ♦ *Children's ownership of the values and rules has been of huge importance to us. There are many ways of accomplishing this and you can feel free to experiment.*
>
> ♦ *Supportive practice with colleagues is also essential. It is important to only do what you are comfortable with and that you have a close and committed team to discuss everything you are doing with. If you are not happy, comfortable, calm, confident and supportive it could be a negative experience for yourself and the children. That defeats the purpose. It is a much better idea to take baby steps and reflect constantly on your journey individually and as a setting.*

Photo: Sue Stokoe

At Nature Nurture children do not need a lot of man-made stuff to play and enjoy themselves. Relationships, freedom to explore and to be trusted are at the heart of the joy of being in wild nature.

Angela Stanton from Alfreton Nursery's advice:

> ◆ *Risk assessment is vital.*
>
> ◆ *Be confident!*
>
> ◆ *Make boundaries explicit.*
>
> ◆ *Be passionate about children's outdoor experiences and learning.*
>
> ◆ *Monitor progress and devise measures to show impact on:*
>
> - *social/emotional well-being*
> - *physical development*
> - *confidence to learn*
> - *language.*
> - *motivation to learn*
>
> ◆ *Ensure a willingness to develop self and others.*
>
> ◆ *Share good practice.*
>
> ◆ *Appropriate clothing for all weathers for staff and children!*

Annette from Abacus Filton Hill Preschool's advice:

> ◆ *Be familiar with the space yourself – go and explore and play first.*
>
> ◆ *Enjoy the experience, keep it simple, children do not need stuff to enjoy.*
>
> ◆ *Step back, watch, listen, learn.*

These young children at Dunblane Nature Kindergarten enjoy revisiting and sharing their experiences on the ipad.

This is advice from just some of the models of children accessing wild nature available in the UK; there are many more centres offering children these valuable opportunities in a variety of different ways. There is no one way that is correct or better, with the underlying philosophy of nature-based practice; practitioners continue to reflect and evolve and try new and different ways of working. What is needed are for more practitioners – like you – advocating for children to be outdoors, to have a sense of the freedom and joy this brings.

Putting it into practice

It takes courage to take that initial leap... now it's time to plan the start of your own journey into wild nature. As many of the practitioners who we interviewed for this book suggested – just do it!

Creating a vision

As we covered in the previous chapter, having a clear vision supports working towards a common goal. Think about the timeframe of your vision:

✿ A short-term vision might be more achievable within a shorter time frame such as all children having access to wild nature for three hours a week.

✿ A long-term vision could be that all children will have daily access to wild nature.

Reflect on and regularly revisit and adapt your vision. Visions can and should be changed and adapted over time; not be set in stone. By constantly reflecting and adapting, children's needs are better catered for.

Finding a suitable site

Wild nature spaces vary greatly from small pockets to large nature reserves, forests, rivers and beaches. Pockets of wild nature can be found in some centres, often fenced off to discourage access. Including these or creating similar spaces within a playground is easily achievable with minimal expense. Initial use of such spaces may be an effective transition with a view to future off-site excursions. Investigate the possibility of using botanical gardens, local parks, sports fields or vacant plots.

Going 'beyond the fence' is exciting and challenging for adults and children alike. The unknown and the oft-forbidden in itself creates adventure. Allowing children to roam out of sight of adults adds an element of risk and challenge, so finding a site that would 'safely' allow children to feel unobserved is recommended – shrubs, trees, hollows and dips could offer this.

A willow arch marks one of the transition spaces from the playground to the wild natural space within the fence at Boldon Nursery School, Outdoor Nursery.

Where to start

A community member might be able to offer access to their farm, forest or coastal property – ideally a site within walking distance, easily accessible on public transport or within a short driving distance. Transport to and from sites is often seen as a major financial or logistical hurdle. Consider asking parents to bring the children to the site and/or collecting them again from the site. Explore the use of community buses not in use at the time – these can often be hired at a minimal cost. It is important to consider the following:

✿ access should be appropriate for all children

✿ children who need mobility aids should have access to appropriate pathways or vehicles

✿ vehicular access for emergency vehicles is imperative

✿ the site you choose should not be environmentally sensitive or protected

✿ be aware of possible hidden seasonal hazards such as floods

✿ is the site on an exposed site subject to lightning strikes?

✿ are you able to adapt the site or your programme when necessary?

Do I need permission?

Seek permission from national parks, local council or landowners as appropriate. Be transparent, familiarise yourself and respect individual wishes as well as nature reserve policies.

How much land do we need?

Although ideal, large tracks of land are not required. Remember, nature-based practice can occur in a section of the playground that has been allowed to grow wild and where native plant species have been reintroduced.

Boldon Nursery School, Outdoor Nursery created a very effective forest site within the existing playground including a tipi and a fire hut.

Shelter

Shelter from the elements is not essential when all are appropriately dressed for the weather. However, having access to a structure would allow some protection in extreme weather, allowing children to warm up and allow storage of equipment. A shelter could be constructed using natural materials and then covered with a tarpaulin when necessary.

Wild toileting

This is often the BIG issue from the adult's perspective. Children deserve to be treated with dignity and offering a sense of privacy in the wild is essential. Access to a nearby public toilet is an option – remember to conduct a thorough risk assessment. Otherwise there are commercial portable toilets. An allocated 'pee' tree or designated area separate from the play space is a simple and effective solution. Solid matter can be collected in a bag to be disposed of off site or buried at least 15 cm deep and 100 metres away from a watercourse. Toilet paper should be bagged and removed from the site.

Using a recycled crate, cutting a hole into the bottom, fixing a child-sized seat with detachable plastic bag and finding a place to offer some privacy was a simple and effective wild toilet for Jenelle Haskew.

Site hazards

It is not necessary to remove natural elements that could pose some risk such as prickly plants, nettles, fungi, cobwebs and sticks. Instead, use these as learning opportunities by supporting children to deal with them.

The biggest hazards are often the man-made hidden dangers. Be aware that public spaces can contain objectionable or potentially hazardous items such as broken glass, condoms and syringes. An advanced site visit will identify problems. Use equipment such as gloves and/or tongs to clean the area.

Involving stakeholders

Practitioners, parents, families, children and the wider community will be the stakeholders and should be involved where possible. It is vital that the entire practitioner team is informed and supportive for such a project to succeed. Include and involve parents and grandparents; it is important that they too contribute their knowledge and views and see the thought, preparation and consideration that is taken.

Including all stakeholders from the outset demonstrates that opinions are valued, which will create a community working together towards the common goal.

Nurturing families and community

As mentioned in the previous section, families and the community have the right to be informed and consulted on any changes or new ventures involving them and their children. Involving parents in the whole process – from reminiscing about childhood experiences, sharing information and research, to the implementation – not only supports parents but also values them as primary caregivers.

A survey could be sent out to families, practitioners and children to gather information. Reflecting on childhood outdoor experiences evokes strong positive emotions with stories of great freedom to explore, being trusted to face and overcome challenges and using found loose parts instead of toys.

Once the survey information is collated and analysed, any initial concerns or doubts can be addressed. Concerns most often link to a perceived increase in risk; include parents in the benefit-risk assessment process, offer opportunities to handle the real tools and invite them to be part of the initial experience to address this concern.

Ensure you clearly articulate why changes are being considered and how these would benefit the children and families, but don't abandon a valuable experience because of a small minority of parents. In exploring risky play Tim Gill (2007) states: 'Don't benchmark down to the parent with the lowest threshold', and I would add, don't benchmark down to the practitioner with the lowest threshold either.

Wild nature committee

It can be hard to do everything on your own. Have an initial meeting with the community to discuss and research the proposed initiative. Form a committee which could consist of members of the local community, parents, staff and children with a special interest in or knowledge about nature.

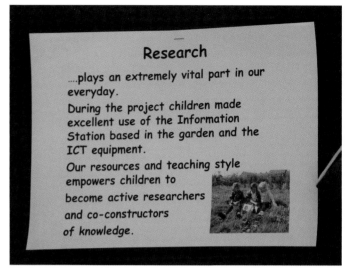

Sharing ethos where practitioners and children are recognised as active researchers is displayed at Boldon Nursery School, Outdoor Nursery.

Adapt centre philosophy, policies and procedures

As a team, review your centre philosophy as well as policies and procedures to include nature-based practice. Include the benefits of children having opportunities to take risks and face challenges. Mention that benefit–risk assessments will be undertaken to weigh up both the benefits and the risks before making a value-based and informed decision on the opportunity.

Continued community involvement

Continue to involve and update all stakeholders after the initial consultations.

* Create a display board sharing experiences, including the benefits. Make the learning visible by linking the experiences to the curriculum, learning and development.

* Share meaningful and visual documentation.

* Include similar information in newsletters and children's reports.

* Invite members of the community to contribute and to join in opportunities.

* Invite local experts to share their expertise with the group.

* Invite the local newspaper to share your journey and raise awareness in the community.

* Have regular social evenings and meetings where families participate in natural experiences such as cooking on fire.

Parent information board sharing the wild nature excursions at Dunblane Nature Kindergarten.

The day's adventures can be shared with the families through rolling slide shows.

Share the benefits

As we've seen, at times the nature-based practice philosophy may be challenged by others, but by sharing your progress and keeping the community up to date with the benefits for the children, practice will be supported and possibly even extended to other children. Share through word of mouth, professional development and swapping of ideas and examples of practice with other practitioners in the wider community.

The Alfreton Nursery School team holds an annual Inset Day for Forest School development, allowing others to experience the benefits. Angela Stanton said of this:

> *This day is invaluable as it provides Forest School training for all, beyond those qualified as Forest School Leaders, so all staff have complete awareness, understanding and skills needed to be able to deliver a passionate Forest Schools curriculum. We also use this day to deliver and create new inspiring ideas, offering governors and other local practitioners the opportunity to join in, learn new skills and be part of creating something inspiring.*

They have also actively involved future teachers by developing an outdoor learning unit of six weeks with a local university for their B.Ed. students: 'Learning outside the classroom', to inspire future teachers. Additionally:

> *We have a lot of visitors who come to see our outdoor provision, and provide courses for the local authority based in our outdoor area. Future plans include a yurt for delivery of training in the woodland, so that practitioners are immersed in the outdoors.*

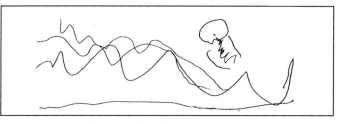

Declan (age four) walking through the long grass.

Influencing change

Children's interests should also influence planning. They are after all very important stakeholders! Fiona Paltridge in Australia shares an example of where the children's fascination prompted change in their centre:

> *Another surprising factor that showed up in children's art work and conversations was the long grass. We have beautiful parks in our town, but when reflecting on why the long grass was so fascinating to the children, we concluded that the parks and homes all have very well-kept, manicured grass areas. This has prompted us to not mow some areas of our outdoor area. Honestly not something we would have thought of.*

Evidence of children's play at Darvell School, left untouched by the adults so that children can come back to them at a later stage. This might be the next day or a few months later.

Regulations, paperwork and other considerations

As with any new venture there will be a number of legal issues and possibly mandatory paperwork to consider. These may sound onerous but the benefits of the experiences you plan to offer the children and the security of completing any required documentation to yourself should far outweigh the initial work involved.

Below I have listed possible considerations; remember there may well be others including centre policies and procedures. Please research the most up-to-date information.

✿ **Benefit-risk assessments:** it is mandatory to complete risk assessments. Chapter 5 looks at the value of weighing up the benefits as well as the risks for specific activities.

✿ **Documentation:** this is important and should be meaningful and accessible to families and children. Below we look at documentation and the preference for photographic records to evidence the learning journey.

✿ **Insurance:** contact your insurer. Providing the benefit–risk assessments and procedures is often all that is required.

✿ **Qualifications:** no specific outdoor or nature-based practice qualification is required. All excursions require an adult with a first-aid qualification. A current advanced or outdoor first-aid training qualification with a specific focus on children is recommended. There are a number of optional qualifications available in the UK which may increase knowledge and confidence; research them and see which would best meet your needs.

✿ **Policies and procedures:** centre policies and procedures are developed by the practitioner team and are not mandatory. There could be some flexibility after discussion if these prevent children from participating in nature-based play. Otherwise follow your setting or service policies and procedures.

✿ **Ratios:** the adult–child ratio is the same as it would be within the setting. As part of our duty of care, the decision on appropriate ratios should be a value-based exercise when doing the benefit–risk assessment and may change depending on the children on the day.

✿ **Group size:** initially practitioners may feel more comfortable taking a small number of the children to a new space. Once everybody feels comfortable, it may be appropriate to extend this opportunity to other children. A group of about 10 to 20 children of mixed ages and abilities forms a very close and inclusive community.

✿ **Length of time:** this may vary from a couple of hours to a whole day. This is a personal and practical decision. There will always be barriers, or perceived barriers, including transport, centre routines and parent pick-up or drop-off. Creative solutions include offering hammocks for tired children, and having parents deliver or pick up children on site may be needed.

Every setting is different; group size, adult-to-child ratios, boundaries, length of time outdoors and opportunities offered are determined by benefit–risk assessments while at the same time considering the duty of care while in the wild environment. Photo taken at Secret Garden, Fife.

Documenting the learning journey in nature-based practice

Meaningful documentation

Meaningful documentation does not mean recording and evidencing everything the children are doing and saying. Practitioners do need to observe, reflect and analyse, but not every observation needs to be recorded in writing or photographed. We can't document everything; use professional judgement and common sense and find a balance.

Why do we need to observe?

✿ To make informed decisions on children's development and their environments.

✿ To retain and share this information with families and colleagues to support children's holistic development.

Some points to ponder when documenting:

✿ Why am I doing this? Who am I doing this for? Is it meaningful to the child and the families?

✿ If we believe that children are instigators of their own learning, is our planning child led?

✿ Have we become obsessive documenters?

✿ A photograph is worth many words, it removes the need for long descriptive text. Unobtrusively photograph the learning journey – children engaged and not cheerfully smiling for the camera. Value photographs taken by the children.

✿ Is the planning cycle evident? Observing, reflecting, analysing, planning, changing the 'environment' and then observing again.

Documentation meaningful to the child and families

Documentation *WITH* and *FOR* children rather than about children is meaningful as children are fully involved in the process. Meaningful documentation:

✿ evidences the process of learning, not only the end product. It records the children's learning journey; their knowledge, ideas, thoughts and understanding are valued, recorded and analysed contextually.

✿ celebrates group documentation. Children learn as a group, bringing diverse knowledge and experiences. This shared information is used by the group to further their knowledge and understanding.

✿ supports children's ownership, using photographs, examples of their own work, including drawings and text and small real objects like leaves and flower petals.

✿ authentically values children's input. Children have access and are able to add new ideas to revise and change previous ideas. They are also able to revisit their learning.

✿ celebrates children's verbal, physical and other 'languages' - Loris Malaguzzi refers to this as the '100 languages of children'.

✿ makes the learning and development visible to families.

✿ evidences observations and reflections that may then inform the planning.

There are many different ways of collecting and collating this information. Select what best reflects your ethos and philosophy while being meaningful to children and families.

The holistic well-being of the child is at the centre of every consideration in nature-based practice. Documentation that takes adults away from the child may not be in the child's best interest. Children do have a right to know what is being documented about them; involving children directly is inclusive and shows that their thinking and interests are valued by the adults.

Learning tracks

I successfully use a documentation framework I have termed
'Learning tracks' which consists of four concise documents
in which information valuable to children and families is
documented:

1. Group project book

(based on the Reggio Emilia and Project Approach)

The Project Approach is a specific kind of project-based
learning dating back to the 1920s (Dewey) sharing in-depth
investigations of children's interests. By documenting such
processes and not end-points, adults evidence and celebrate
what children are able to do, demonstrating competence.
Significantly, over time, progression in learning, development,
abilities and skills are evidenced through skilled practitioners
identifying and making the learning and development visible
through the use of appropriate keywords. This documentation is
created with the children.

2. Individual children's portfolios

These contain a collection of documents that evidence children's
learning and development through 'Learning stories' (Margaret
Carr and Wendy Lee), photographs of relevant experiences
documented in the group project book, observations, reflections,
artwork, photographs etc.

3. Community sharing book

A book sharing meaningful community information with
families including research, relevant news articles, practitioner
professional development and community involvement.

4. Planning and reflection file

Evidences child-led planning and a weekly critical reflection
informing future practice.

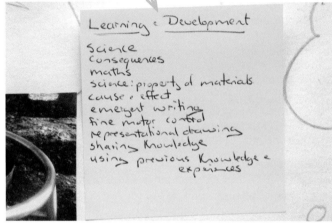

*A group project book exploring the children's interest in fire. Finding out what
children know about fire forms the baseline assessment; the journey into the
investigations of fire is formatively assessed throughout and may culminate
in a summative assessment of their increased knowledge. Significantly, the
learning and development evidenced in these play-based investigations are
identified by the practitioner and documented using keywords. This is one
engaging way of making the learning visible to families.*

NBP in action

PROBLEM SOLVING

A five-year-old boy found a stick
approximately 20 cm long, added his
marshmallow and held it over the fire. He
soon experienced the discomfort of such
a short stick, his fingers getting hot and
smoke rising into his eyes. He left the fire
and returned having solved the problem
himself by extending the marshmallow
stick, attaching a longer stick using metal
wire. He then discovered that his stronger
stick could now hold two marshmallows –
an added bonus..

A contextual problem-solving opportunity that involves maths, science, engineering and technology.

Let's get going

Now that you have formed your vision, done your research, made your decisions and done the necessary paperwork, you are ready for this exciting adventure! To do this you might need to push yourself out of your comfort zone and be a risk taker; there is only so much preparation you can do before you need to actually get out there and just do it. Remember, you can always make changes and adaptations.

Introducing the concept

Establish children's existing experience or knowledge of nature play. Camping with family and friends, fishing in rivers, time spent on farms or family holidays at the seaside could be shared. What did they enjoy about these spaces? What did they do?

Establish boundaries and expected behaviour, consulting with the children and coming to agreements; such agreements are more effective than adults presenting children with a long list of rules. I advise that only three agreements are needed:

1. Try not to hurt yourself.

2. Try not to hurt anybody else.

3. Try not to damage property.

Call a short 'meeting' just before the excursion to discuss the expected routines and events of the day. Explain that there will be another short meeting once at the site to agree the boundaries before children will be free to explore.

Arrival

Reaching the identified site may involve walking a considerable distance. Children lead the way with agreed regular waiting places – these are again identified by the children and could be a rock, tree or hole, often aptly named by the children. Initially these next waiting places should be within sight; later you may be happy with 'skipping' a waiting place when everyone feels comfortable with being out of sight and children reliably wait.

The journey to the settling site is not rushed, children running ahead to the next waiting place are expected to wait, play, climb, explore or rest until everybody has caught up and the next waiting place has been agreed on. Common sense, dynamic risk assessments and educator knowledge play a large role in such decisions.

On reaching the settling site, a short safety meeting takes place, and adults and children may initially walk around the boundary to familiarise themselves after a period of absence. Don't rush. Point out landmarks so that children will recognise the boundaries themselves. Keep it simple and, where possible, use natural landmarks such as a track, a dry riverbed, a fallen tree. Ensure that the boundaries are well within the adult comfort zone. Children will on occasion forget or push these limits, so having a second ring of safety is reassuring.

Practitioners may initially feel more comfortable with a smaller space, extending the area children can explore after a few visits.

The best safety meetings are short, relevant and have maximum engagement – you might not get it right all the time.

Wild nature session

Children explore and discover in their own time and at their own pace. Adults may demonstrate a specific skill, answer children's questions accurately and scaffold opportunities. At the end of a session, adults and children wind down, reflect and share thoughts and ideas. What was the best bit? Were there any bits that were not so good? What would we change and what do we need to remember for the next time?

Considering and adapting for individual circumstances

No two settings will be the same, nor will they have the same requirements when it comes to nature-based practice. The actual practice or pedagogy in wild nature does not change although practitioners' experience, skill and knowledge may need to adapt.

A knowledge of tidal patterns, sea creatures and water hazards would be important when taking children to the beach or river but not relevant in the forest. A good knowledge of the natural space is important; research local fauna and flora and site specific hazards before venturing out with the children.

Practitioners may initially choose to take visual prompts supporting the engagement of some children who struggle to relate to a new environment.

What to take with you

Definitely not as much as possible! Equipment can be transported by car, bus, trolley or in backpacks with children taking responsibility. What you take depends on the site you are visiting, the length of time you will be there and your philosophy.

Essentials

Our duty of care is paramount, and some equipment could be considered essential for the welfare of the group:

- ✿ Mobile phone with emergency numbers. The group should always be contactable and able to contact others in an emergency. Know where reception is available and ensure that others know where you can be found in an emergency.

- ✿ First-aid kit appropriate for the site you are accessing.

- ✿ Drinking water. Children can carry their own water bottles but adults need to bring additional water.

- ✿ Water to wash hands. Water and friction is all that is needed to wash hands unless children have had contact with infectious material.

- ✿ ID cards for every child and adult in the group. These are small laminated cards with emergency contact numbers, medical conditions, medication and photograph.

- ✿ Individual essential medication. For example: EpiPen, asthma and epilepsy medication.

- ✿ Appropriate clothing and footwear with a spare set.

- ✿ Sun protection to protect from UV rays. For example, sun cream and hats.

- ✿ Healthy snack.

Children from the age of about two years can carry their own backpacks with the equipment, food and water necessary for the day.

Important

Additional resources or equipment that are more site and weather specific:

- ✿ Spare clothing. Include a spare sunhat on sunny days and spare warm hat/coat for cold days for the group.

- ✿ Camera/iPad. Children may want to record what is important to them while adults use this as a recording and assessment tool.

- ✿ Shelter if there is no natural protection. A tarpaulin can be used to create shade or used to offer some protection from rain.

- ✿ Gloves and/or tongs to pick up litter and other hazardous objects as well as a plastic bag to collect this in.

- ✿ Toilet paper and plastic bags.

- ✿ Insect repellent.

Recommended

There are no hard and fast 'rules'. Individual philosophy and vision should inform practice; the priority is to ensure that the opportunities offered are beneficial and developmentally appropriate. The ages and developmental stages of the children, how regularly they attend sessions, how experienced they are, the length of the sessions are all factors that may influence decisions.

Appropriate tools:

- ✿ whittlers to remove the bark of green sticks and shape a point on a stick
- ✿ junior hacksaws to saw through small sticks
- ✿ hand drills to drill holes into wood
- ✿ hammers or preferably wooden mallets to knock sticks into the ground
- ✿ assortment of wood files
- ✿ wire cutters to cut wire for construction or lashing
- ✿ fire steel to start the cooking fire
- ✿ secateurs to cut small branches
- ✿ loppers to cut branches up to 20 cm in diameter
- ✿ bowsaw to saw larger branches for use by older children or adult-guided use with younger children.

Tools appropriate for use by the age and developmental stage of the children.

Other appropriate equipment:

- ✿ gloves to be worn only on the hand not holding the tool (saws)
- ✿ safety goggles when sawing above the head
- ✿ tape measures
- ✿ twine, soft florist wire, ropes to lash with
- ✿ sandpaper
- ✿ cotton wool and Vaseline as a fire starter
- ✿ fire blanket
- ✿ relevant reference books
- ✿ container to hold water near the fire
- ✿ pencils and notepads for children and adult use.

Man-made materials such as wire to hold together constructions will need to be removed from the space to protect wildlife.

Preferably not

Experiences in wild nature are different, with new levels of adventure, excitement and challenge, not replicas of what is offered in the playground or classroom.

I don't consider these resources appropriate, as natural alternatives are available:

- ✿ toys
- ✿ computer games
- ✿ plastic tools
- ✿ jigsaw puzzles
- ✿ manufactured building blocks
- ✿ dressing-up clothes
- ✿ poster paint.

You decide what to take

The resources and opportunities available to the children are likely to reflect practitioners' beliefs. Where to draw the line is a personal decision: catching, killing and cooking your own food or taking along food to cook? Using only hands, feet, teeth and found objects to manipulate materials or taking along appropriate tools?

Nature-based practice is not so much about survivalist experiences but rather being and learning with nature. The place of 'tools' that can be used in nature-based practice remains a personal choice. Keep an open mind, use what is appropriate for you, your children and your environment.

The place of tools

To take tools or not to take tools? This has been debated by various groups and depends on personal preference. If children are going out for regular, long periods of time, they may reach a stage in their play where there needs to be some form of progression to increase independence and challenge; this could be introduced in the form of appropriate tools.

As I mentioned above, I don't advocate taking plastic cups and saucers, dressing-up clothes or paint, but from experience have found that taking limited manufactured resources can extend and enrich children's experiences. For example, saws will increase independence and allow children to cut larger sticks to the length they need. (See above for recommended tools.)

Being able to choose the right tool to cut the stick into different lengths enables this boy to make his own outdoor xylophone.

The place of information technology

While children are not encouraged to sit under a tree playing computer games, there are many benefits to using digital technology. Using a digital camera to take a photograph of a spider from a safe distance then enlarging it to see the detail is scarily exciting.

Providing children with cameras to share their perspective is a valuable consultative tool for both verbal and non-verbal children of all ages when the images are shared, analysed and reflected on. It is exciting that nature can be celebrated through hands-on authentic experiences and linked to technologies that are accessible.

Scarily exciting bull ants guarding their nest in Australia. Those pincers cause a painful nip - I have experience! Fortunately these are not found in the UK.

'I took a picture of the world.'

NBP in action

THROUGH THE CHILD'S LENS

Fiona Paltridge in Australia talks about the children's use of cameras during their nature excursions:

Their perspectives are unique and often amaze us, from capturing the 'crunchy leaves' under their feet to the reflections of the trees in the car window. Not only have their observations given us heaps to take back and revisit in our centre but also an insight into the thinking of these amazing young minds.

Admittedly we go through a LOT of cameras and video recorders, but the results are worth it. Digital cameras, flip cameras and video cameras are all used by the children confidently and correctly. Of course it took a little bit of practice but now they are better at it than we are.

Appropriate IT options for nature-based practice:

- ❀ digital cameras to photograph the environment and each other, as well as to document and share
- ❀ digital microscopes attached to laptops or computers in the centre to look closely at leaves, bugs, water and soil
- ❀ iPads to research, photograph, write and share information onsite
- ❀ sound recorders to record the sounds of birds, the wind, 'silence'
- ❀ night-vision cameras to record nocturnal activities
- ❀ digital video recorder in bird boxes to see and hear the birds
- ❀ smart phones with appropriate apps to identify seeds, trees, and animals
- ❀ video cameras to film the action and children's voices.

Having children use cameras on their own opens up windows to their thinking. They capture what is important to them at that moment and then share it with family and friends. It allows valuable community connections linking wild nature, the centre and home.

The place of fire

Does fire have a place in nature-based practice? Fire is one of the natural elements so it could certainly be considered as an appropriate experience. Humans have had a very close connection to fire for centuries; we still use fire in celebrations, and gathering around a campfire creates a tribal sense of community.

Adults often react with horror when childcare and fire are mentioned together. Is it our place as practitioners to introduce children to the benefits and dangers of fire? Here I agree with Bob Hughes that monitored fire play in such supervised environments is appropriate.

> *Playgrounds are ideal environments for intelligently-monitored fire play. Children are not stupid; nor do they knowingly endanger themselves under normal circumstances. By developing a real interaction with fire, in conjunction with safety practices, children can learn about the uses of fire first hand.*
>
> Hughes, 1996

Developing a healthy respect and knowledge of fire is a life skill. It is better for children to do this in a supervised environment where skilled adults are monitoring, than secretly when adults are not around – under the bed, behind the shed or in the forest.

Larger fires allow children to build on previous knowledge of small fires and to explore additional concepts as this boy at Riverside Cottage Nursery is discovering when cooking apples.

A young boy exploring the properties of fire through making and maintaining a small fire in a supervised environment. His fascination with fire is supported as he learns about concepts such as combustion, heat, fire safety and putting the fire out.

A community of learning and teaching

Children are natural scientists and are instinctively curious, actively theorising and seeking answers to their questions. Adults are not the holders of all knowledge; children are profound thinkers and may ask questions to which there may not immediately be an answer. Celebrate children's thinking and hypothesise; it is not so much about the correct answer but the actual thinking.

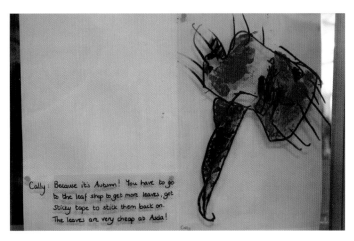

Chloe: The tree picks up the leaves with its sticks (branches). It bends down to pick up the leaves.

Cally: Because it's Autumn! You have to go to the leaf shop to get more leaves, get sticky tape to stick them back on. The leaves are very cheap at Asda!

These young children's framework of understanding about autumn leaves is highly complex and informed through prior knowledge or experience. Wingate Nursery School celebrated their thinking with families through an attractive window display.

A practitioner asked three- and four-year-old children: '*I wonder why there are so many leaves on the ground?*' The children's responses were varied and imaginative:

'*Because the tree doesn't want them any more.*'

'*Maybe they are too heavy to stay up there?*'

'*I think they wanted to come down so we could collect them.*'

Should she have corrected them and taught them all about autumn leaves? My inclination would be to encourage further thinking and conversations about trees and leaves rather than correcting them – which in essence is telling them their thinking is wrong.

> *When you teach a child something, you take away forever his chance of discovering it for himself.*
>
> Piaget

The thrill of finding a snail by yourself is so much greater than coming to look at one the practitioner has found. Providing an exciting environment such as the natural environment and then showing children the surprises is like giving them a present and then unwrapping it yourself.

A collaborative learning approach

In nature-based practice children are viewed as decision-makers where discussions are held and agreements are reached. The following example of this approach uses the introduction of fire.

Introducing fire

Sharing prior knowledge

Establish children's existing knowledge about the topic. What do they already know about fire? How are fires started; how can they be extinguished? It might be a family or cultural tradition to have regular fires around the home; they may have had experience of campfires.

Once this baseline knowledge has been established, children's knowledge and thinking can be extended through experience, teaching specific skills, and prompts such as verbal comments or questions, modelling opportunities, photographs and real objects.

Children's thinking is documented to share with families and allow children to revisit their experiences and thinking over time.

Supporting children's thinking

Support and guide children's thinking about possible hazards, risks and the procedures linked to fires. Some less obvious points to consider:

- ✿ **Denudation:** be aware of the environmental impact when collecting wood for the fire. Wood might have to be brought in.
- ✿ **Fire restrictions:** ensure that there are no restrictions to lighting a fire.
- ✿ **Permission:** seek permission from the landowner.
- ✿ **Space:** make sure there are no overhanging branches or roots that can catch fire.
- ✿ **Benefit-risk assessment:** completed by adults and children; closely follow the agreed procedures.

At the Secret Garden in Fife fire plays an important role; keeping children warm, cooking a nourishing soup and drying damp clothing.

Safety around the fire

❀ Create a fire circle. Depending on the size of the fire, visually mark the high-risk area using sitting logs, rope. For a large fire on the ground this circle would be approximately 1.5 m from the fire; for smaller fires use professional judgement and common sense.

❀ Raise awareness and remove all trip hazards such as sticks, roots, tools and equipment from the fire circle.

❀ Agree on appropriate clothing and footwear.

❀ Once the fire is lit, agree on no running or playing within the fire circle and walking behind the fire circle if necessary to move.

❀ Initially adults may want to 'invite' children into the circle to add wood or cook, allowing close monitoring.

❀ Ensure that all procedures are closely followed and fire blanket/ fire extinguisher/sand/water are close to hand.

❀ Make sure that a source of cold water is close in the unlikely event of burns and scalds.

Small world fire display enables children at Nature Nurture to practise and explore campfires in play.

Fire first aid

❀ It is the responsibility of all adults to be aware of the most up to date advice on burns, as best advice may change.

❀ Burns should immediately be immersed in cold/tepid running water for at least 20 minutes; stirring a bucket of water is a good option.

❀ Only remove clothing that isn't stuck to the burn once the burn is cooled off.

❀ Burns larger than the child's hand size need urgent medical attention.

❀ Do not cover with any creams or lotions. Cling film/wrap can be used to protect the wound after thorough cooling.

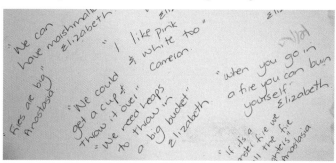

Young children develop a good knowledge of keeping safe near fire through carefully guided procedures introduced by adults.

Cooking on fire

❀ Food coming off the fire is likely to be very hot and could cause a painful burn.

❀ Be aware of others around; try not touch others with hot food.

❀ Never test the temperature of the food using the mouth or lips; test with fingers after allowing a cooling-off period (younger children are encouraged to count to ten before testing with their fingers).

Some children, in their excitement, may need to be reminded that food coming off the fire will be hot.

Putting fires out

❀ Candle fires can be blown out. Larger fires need to be deprived of oxygen. Some children may not be aware of this if their only experience is birthday candles.

❀ Water can be poured on a fire to extinguish it. Raise awareness that this could add the additional hazard of scalding when the water changes into steam.

❀ Placing damp soil onto the fire is a safe way of extinguishing a small fire when children are in the vicinity. Follow up with water when appropriate. Dry sand will retain the heat and the fire could reignite, so is not appropriate.

❀ Discuss the appropriate use of the available water bucket, fire blanket and fire extinguishers.

❀ Ensure there is no chance of the fire reigniting. It is good practice to remove all evidence of fire-making unless the fire was made in an already designated space. This is to discourage others making fires without landowner permission.

Pouring water on the fire to extinguish it gives the child a sense of empowerment. Working with small fires allows young children to be fully involved in the whole process and reduces some of the risks associated with larger fires.

Let's make a fire!

Ready – practising

✿ Enable children to practise with pretend fires and candles.

✿ Introduce lit candles under supervision. Feel the heat above the flame. Talk about how the air too is hot and can burn the skin.

✿ Collect wood, stack it, clear a fire circle of trip hazards and practise not walking through this circle when changing position.

✿ Place a lit candle into the pretend fire; offer the opportunity to really practise – this is starting to get exciting.

Steady – preparing

Decide on the type of fire you need: a small one to cook a few marshmallows or a larger one to cook bread?

Fire container:

✿ small fires: a commercial fire bowl, old frying pan, stainless steel bowl, metal colander, cleared ground space.

✿ large raised fire: freestanding above-ground barbecue (some have a safety ring that doesn't heat), a raised, purpose-built fire pit.

✿ large ground level fire: a sunken or ground-level fire pit with log or stone surround. Ensure stones will not crack in the heat and cause injuries.

Making a small individual fire in an inexpensive stainless steel bowl gives a child or a small group of children ownership over 'their' fire.

Firewood:

✿ Collect: wood needs to be dry to burn effectively – collect from fallen branches, using parts not on the ground when the ground is damp.

✿ Sort: by size and length using non-standard measurements – as long as the distance between your hand and your elbow, as long as your hand, as long as your little finger.

✿ Arrange: larger pieces are at the bottom, smaller pieces and the kindling at the top or arrange into a tee-pee shape surrounding small kindling. Ensure that air can flow freely.

Collecting and sorting sticks through a variety of criteria is engaging and offers another mathematics and science learning opportunity.

Pyramid fire ready to be lit with thickest wood at the bottom, small kindling placed on top and then surrounded by medium kindling placed in a tee pee format.

Go – lighting the fire

Fire lighting in itself is an ancient craft and children are fascinated by the more challenging ways of lighting a fire, often trying to rub sticks together which is unlikely to produce satisfactory results. Matches and lighters are easy and boring in comparison and do not require the skill of other more traditional methods.

IGNITING THE SPARK

A child at Urafirth Primary School on the Shetland Islands enthusiastically shared his knowledge of traditional fire lighting by rubbing two sticks together. When he did not succeed he reflected, adjusted the angles of the sticks, the kindling, the tempo. Other children offered support and advice and it was decided that the fire would not light because the sticks were damp and that matches or a lighter were needed. At this point a fire steel was offered. The children practised with renewed enthusiasm and shouted in delight when the first sparks were produced. A communal cheer was heard when sparks eventually lit a fire and children could not wait for embers to form before melting marshmallows and chocolate on sticks and spoons shaped by themselves.

Reflection of learning and development: FUN, perseverance, resilience, science, sharing prior knowledge, developing new concepts, mathematics, co-operation, fine and gross motor development, problem solving, creative thinking, risk taking, engineering, technology, confidence, self-esteem, co-ordination, manual dexterity, literacy, sharing... the list is endless!

Planning possibilities:

✿ explore history of fire lighting using reference books/website

✿ investigate the technology behind fire steels, matches, fire lighters, flints

✿ children reflect and document their experiences

✿ explore appropriate tools for cooking on fire through conduction of heat

✿ collect recipes that can be cooked on fire

✿ explore the benefits of fire

✿ explore combustion – why did the fire of London not burn down the churches?

Using a fire steel is challenging; children have a real sense of achievement when they firstly make a spark and secondly when that spark starts the fire. Using dry tinder and a fire-lighter guarantees a degree of success after the effort. Vaseline (petroleum product) on a piece of cottonwool is a very effective and inexpensive firelighter.

An 18-month-old lacks the manual dexterity to successfully light the fire but has a sense of achievement when scraping along the metal.

A five-year-old effectively using the fire steel after practice has the manual dexterity and perseverance to successfully and responsibly light a fire.

✿ Embers: glow red when blown on but will not burst into flames and need contact with tinder which will ignite and burn.

✿ Natural tinder: fine dry material which ignites easily; plant material such as small leaves and fine grass can be rubbed between the fingers to make it fine. Dry grass can be folded into a small 'tinder bundle' or nest.

✿ Fire starter: small pad of cottonwool dipped in petroleum jelly placed on the kindling ready for the spark is not a necessity but offers faster 'success'.

✿ Feeding the fire: adults monitor; could be a hazard while children are still inexperienced.

Introducing tools

Gather the children for a 'meeting' and introduce the tools one at a time; find out what they know about each one. Encourage them to think about appropriate use of the tool and keeping safe. Document this for the benefit-risk assessments. Reach agreement on safe use and maintenance of tools and encourage the children to suggest sanctions to be implemented should children 'forget' the agreed process. Having to replace the tool until a later stage is sufficient, although the children themselves may come up with rather severe sanctions that may need to be tempered. TIP: reassure them; do not scare them. These tools are safe and we don't want children to be fearful of their lives using a whittler or junior hacksaw.

A wood file, whittler, hand drills and junior hacksaw are appropriate tools for toddlers and children of all ages. Gloves are not worn on the hand holding the tool to enable to child to have maximum control of the tool.

Demonstrating and emphasising safety points

To support all learning styles demonstrate using the tools through actions and sounds.

- ✿ Whittler: show children how to peel the bark off a green stick by pushing the peeler away from the hand holding the stick. Pretend to forget and pull it towards the hand nearly 'peeling' yourself (actions and sound effects without being overly dramatic). Ask the children what they think you are doing wrong. They will tell you to push it away from your body. Emphasise the correct actions again.

- ✿ Junior hacksaw: hold a stick in one hand and saw with the other. Pretend to let the saw slip and accidentally nick your hand (action and noise effects). Ask the children what safety measures you could take and they will tell you to either keep your hand further away from the saw or to put a glove on the hand holding the branch, the non-tool hand.

- ✿ If children need to move the tool away from the tool zone, they should walk slowly holding the tool down next to the body.

- ✿ No tools may be left on the ground and all need to be returned as soon as the child is finished.

- ✿ The child doing the sawing should hold their own wood.

- ✿ Do not get too close to a child with a tool. Stay out of the tool user's 'blood-bubble', the space the tool could reach.

- ✿ Any other safety measures you feel are necessary but keep them to a minimum – we are not talking chainsaws and power tools here.

Dealing with parental concerns

In the previous chapter, areas that parents often have concerns about were discussed. Here are some ways of allaying these parental concerns.

Sharing through site visits

Practitioners welcome families to spend time with their children on location. This allows parents to really know what is being offered and often takes the angst of the unknown away. Some parents enjoy it so much they come back to the site during the weekend. One parent with concerns about a small stream joined the group and later commented:

> *I'm also really glad I came along. I would encourage anyone who has any fears about the safety of the area to go along. It was so reassuring to see your safety routines and how tame the waters are.*

The fear of the unknown is often reduced when parents are able to participate in the experiences.

Once children are experienced, additional tools may be introduced either within the setting or in the natural wild space. Competent children at Darvell School safely use a large range of tools for functional as well as creative opportunities.

Sharing through documentation

Many practitioners felt that sharing the opportunities children had through documenting and taking photographs allowed families to be part of the experiences. Some childminders share information on private social media sites allowing families to share the journeys with them on a week-to-week basis.

A mutual trust must be established. Parents also want the best for their children, so there is a common goal, and sharing practice with families reassures them of this.

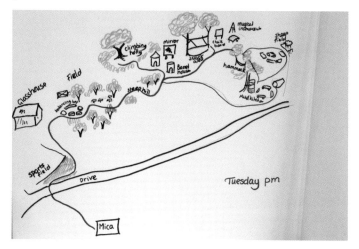

Nature Nurture share their physical journey through documentation in a book which can be revisited.

Dunblane Nature Kindergarten displays children's delight in exploring mud. This display can be transferred into a group project book to allow continued access.

Boldon Nursery School, Outdoor Nursery created a 3D display with photographs, artefacts and group art work celebrating their exploration into seasonal berries.

Parental feedback

Parental feedback should inform future practice. It is important that practitioners are responsive to parental feedback to build trust. Many practitioners reported that families were now undertaking similar excursions with their children, which is great testimony to the value of these projects.

Gathering and sharing feedback from families is valuable to staff, families and visitors. Here families at Boldon Nursery School, Outdoor Nursery shared some of their views about the nursery as part of a silk wall-hanging display.

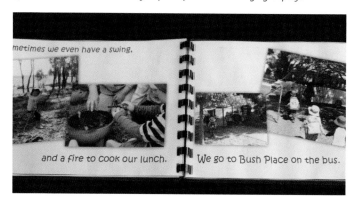

A parent in Australia suggested that a social story before children go out may be helpful so that they know what to expect. In response, the team created photo booklets that can be accessed in the centre to prepare children for the excursion.

Angela Green of Child First Northampton shared this positive feedback from a parent:

> *Our son has attended Child First from 14 months old and we can honestly say that he has not only extremely enjoyed his time at the nursery, but has developed and advanced in to a beautiful caring boy. His desire to be outside is truly evident as he loves to be in the garden exploring and this is all down to the wonderful Forest School programme the nursery introduces to the children. The free flow approach has allowed our son to thrive and focus on activities he truly enjoys, which he always seems so excited to share with us at the end of each day.*
>
> *The facilities, inspirational staff and outdoor space have all attributed to preparing our son for his next steps in life.*
>
> *(Father)*

Assessment and registration visits

The current regulating bodies fully support and encourage settings to offer children regular access to the outdoors including wild natural environments embracing risk and challenge. The table below adapted from the document *My World Outdoors* (Care Inspectorate), illustrates the higher rate of 'excellent' grades awarded by theme to outdoor-based services on 31st August 2015.

	Awarded EXCELLENT in the theme, Quality of:			
	Care and Support	Environment	Staffing	Management and Leadership
% of outdoor-based services (grade 6)	17%	17%	17%	8%
% of children's daycare services nationally (grade 6)	6%	3%	5%	4%

Annette from Abacus Filton Hill Nursery, reflected on how such experiences may not be familiar to some:

> *They cannot bring their laptops with them! They have to use their eyes and ears; it can be a new experience for this person too!*

Filton Hill Preschool was rated 'outstanding' by Ofsted in 2015.

Child First Northampton was rated 'outstanding' by Ofsted in 2013 with positive comments about the outdoor opportunities provided:

> • *The nursery grounds are a rich learning environment. Children enjoy a wealth of opportunities to expand their imagination and understanding of the world and to develop physically and emotionally.*
>
> • *Parents comment that they are 'over the moon' with how their children are progressing and that they and their children 'thoroughly enjoy the nursery experience'.*
>
> • *For large periods of each day, children experience the awe and wonder of playing in the grounds and woods. They pick runner beans and strawberries with their friends and run amongst the trees to find, then get away from the dancing monster. Babies have their own secure outdoor area which is ideal for those who are not yet mobile. Older babies have supervised visits to larger play areas when it is less busy, so start to experience the excitement of the outside environment which is such an asset to this nursery.*

Orchard Nature Nursery:

> *Opportunities for outdoor play were particularly good in this nursery. Children were able to engage in physical, energetic play outdoors throughout the day and in all weathers. The children knew the routine for preparing for outdoor play and independently accessed appropriate clothing and footwear to ensure they were warm and dry. Children were independent and confident in the natural environment. They had opportunities to promote their creativity and imagination and to stimulate and challenge them. Some children talked confidently about making popcorn on the fire pit and about how they had to be responsible and ensure they were safe.*

Riverside Cottage Nursery:

> *Very positive on the whole - particularly so recently. Using the outdoors and encouraging outdoor nurseries has been a massive (and really quite sudden) approach for the Care Inspectorate. We have actually been working with them to produce a new document called My World Outdoors (April 2016) which is designed to highlight best practice and bring attention to the outdoors as the perfect place to implement it.*

Nature Nurture:

> *Care Inspectorate and Education Scotland have visited as part of their inspection of Camphill School Aberdeen. They were very impressed.*

Alfreton Nursery School:

> *Ofsted commented in our latest outstanding judgement 2015, (www.alfreton.derbyshire.sch.uk): Children make particularly rapid progress in their physical development, with the majority reaching skills beyond those expected for their age when they leave. The exemplary outdoor areas help children become increasingly confident in challenging their bodies while running, jumping, climbing and balancing on different surfaces. The high quality 'Forest School' areas enable children to make excellent progress in their skills in exploring, investigating and learning about the natural world.*

Boldon Nursery School, Outdoor Nursery:

> *Whilst working this way we have had two OFSTED inspections, both resulting in outstanding in all areas. The most recent inspection was March 2015.*

In the inspection report the benefits of the nature-based practice within the school was clearly identified.

Secret Garden, Scotland, was the first application received to register a nursery running solely in a woodland without traditional premises. Since then the regulator has supported the development of a range of other outdoors-only provision.

> • *The curriculum is extremely stimulating, incorporating a broad range of rich inspiring, varied and creative experiences. The statement, 'the best classroom and richest cupboard is roofed only by the sky', underpins the school's ethos and drive to use nature and the seasons to stimulate children's curiosity and enhance their learning. This includes in their early reading, writing and mathematical work.*
>
> • *The behaviour of the children is outstanding. Children are highly motivated and keen to learn. They play and learn together happily and highly successfully.*
>
> • *The children show an exceptional awareness for their age of how to keep themselves safe. They are quick to identify risk and danger in potentially tricky situations, such as when using the tyre swing, climbing a tree or pouring themselves a cup of warm chocolate in the outdoor cabin. Children learn crucial skills of balance, coordination and providing a helping hand to a friend quickly.*
>
> • *Children's early reading, writing and mathematical skills are developed exceptionally well because frequent practice of these essential skills is firmly embedded through everyday activities. For example, staff skilfully develop children's grasp of number, counting and measuring in the mud kitchen, counting out pieces of pasta and measuring quantities of split peas and sand to form their mixture.*
>
> • *Speaking and listening skills are developed rapidly. Staff successfully give confidence to children to express their feelings, emotions and thoughts. For example, after composing and acting out a story outdoors, such as building a rocket with tyres to fly into space to recover a jewel, children are encouraged to write some of the key words from the story when they return indoors to the studio.*
>
> • *The imaginative and extremely stimulating environments both inside and outdoors, and the inventive match of activities to capture and hold interest, enable children to make rapid progress and achieve exceptionally well. This was evident when birds of prey were brought into school. When questioned, children described essential features of the barn owl, such as their size, feather colour and shape, in detail. They of course recognised the barn owl from some of their favourite stories, such as those involving the adventures of the Gruffalo.*

My best advice is to welcome all visitors to the environment, be confident and articulate in sharing the learning, benefits and children's experience with them. Know why you are offering these opportunities and share your setting's philosophy, policies, procedures and benefit–risk assessments that reflect your practice.

Pushing boundaries and following a vision that is not mainstream can be lonely. Having a supportive team, network and service is not only inspiring but also leads to expanding visions and philosophies.

An Information Station in one of the outdoor cabins at Boldon Nursery School offers children access to relevant reference books, magnifying glasses and other resources to support curiosity and independent investigation.

Chapter 5

Risks and challenges

Academic learning, regulations and risks are the three most common barriers mentioned when discussing taking children into the natural environment. For many, these hurdles are great and problematic. Others wish to offer such opportunities and strive to overcome any hurdles. None of these challenges need restrict children having access to wild nature.

Learning with nature

> *Societal priorities for young children – safety and school readiness – may be hindering children's physical development.'*
>
> Copeland et al., 2012

As we've seen already, learning does not have to happen within a walled classroom, even for our 12-year-olds. The child is not the curriculum. Whatever curriculum we use, it does not change the value of children having access to nature – their need to be in nature remains. Fortunately, our curricula are flexible, and high outcomes can be achieved in a range of places and ways. In Scotland the Care Inspectorate has published the document, *My World Outdoors*, sharing good practice in how early years services can provide play and learning wholly or partially outdoors. I have highlighted the fact that all play and learning could occur outdoors.

At Riverside Cottage children are given a lot of space and freedom to explore and make their own way to different sites outside the grounds. This level of confidence comes with knowing and trusting the children in your care and communicating clear expectations and boundaries to all.

No time to go and play

There is often a perception that children will be 'left behind' — that they are not learning unless they are sitting at a desk being instructed. Due to this misconception many children are not allowed to be carefree, to experience the joy of play. There is often no time to just 'be' and to 'go and play' freely as academic pressure takes precedence.

Play is free, exploratory, joyous and child-led. It is not a luxury, but remains an essential for children and adults alike. Children's dispositions for learning through play should be valued and prioritised, and one of the roles of practitioners is making the learning obvious to others when children are playing.

In nature children's natural dispositions for learning; curiosity and wonder, are fuelled as they explore the sensory environment on offer.

good co
to agre
was de

After seeing the children's fascination with investigating the puddle depth we decided to further their intrest by exploring the different depths of the river.....

Again we use a stick to place into the water to check the water depth marking it with a pen. The children help to measure three different point of the river the edge, middle and far away edge.....

Dunblane Nature Kindergarten makes the learning that happens when children play visible to the parents through notice boards; on this board contextual maths opportunities are highlighted.

The curriculum in nature

This is based on research and theories. The belief that children are capable and competent learners drives practitioners' programmes and allows children to participate in developmentally appropriate opportunities, including challenges, as offered in nature-based practice.

Nature-based practice supports the Principles of the National Care Standards:

✿ dignity and respect

✿ compassion

✿ inclusivity

✿ responsive care and support

✿ well-being.

Nature-based practice supports the Principles of the Early Years Foundation Stage (EYFS):

✿ unique child

✿ positive relationships

✿ enabling environments

✿ learning and development.

Learning outcomes

These are skills, knowledge or dispositions that can be actively promoted by practitioners in collaboration with children and families. Children show:

✿ a strong sense of identity when they feel safe and secure and feel confident in exploring new challenges.

✿ connectedness and they contribute to the world when they respect the natural environment, work together in a group, respect diversity and are aware of fairness.

✿ a strong sense of well-being as they are able to self-risk assess and are aware of the emotional and physical benefits of being outdoors.

✿ that they are confident and involved learners as their curiosity and interest in the environment drives them to find out more. They explore concepts and ideas through play, using imagination and creativity.

✿ that they are effective communicators as they share knowledge with each other verbally and non-verbally. They use cameras and reference books to explore and share interests.

'Look, I picked it – roots!' this little girl at Riverside Cottage is curious about the natural world around her.

Dispositions for learning

Nature-based practice supports the nine dispositions for learning, promoting a love for learning.

✿ **Curiosity:** comes naturally to children in an environment that is unpredictable and changeable, such as the forest, stream or beach.

✿ **Enthusiasm:** through their own curiosity, discovering a 'new' natural world, together with passionate practitioners, children remain enthralled with a sense of wonder.

✿ **Cooperation:** playing together, listening, sharing, and taking turns. In an ever-changing natural space children naturally tend to work together.

✿ **Confidence:** children who are valued as the decision makers will have increased confidence in their own abilities.

✿ **Creativity:** supporting children in expressing their own ideas in nature art, including stories and music, encourages personal natural creativity.

✿ **Commitment:** children become involved in matters that interest them while exploring in nature, and with this comes commitment to their interest.

✿ **Persistence:** being committed will drive children to complete their self-chosen task, even when challenging.

✿ **Imagination:** open-ended natural materials will stimulate children's imagination. Adults who respect and value their ideas, who allow them time and space, will encourage greater imagination.

✿ **Reflectivity:** thinking and sharing their exciting natural experiences with adults who support thinking rather than directing or teaching. Documentation that allows children to come back to and add to their experiences enables them to reflect on their own experiences and learning.

Regulations

As practitioners recognise the limits of playgrounds and the benefits of natural spaces, many are introducing regular wild nature outings beyond the fence. There is nothing in the regulations that should prevent practitioners from offering this. There is no specific legislation on play safety in the UK, and undertaking a 'suitable and sufficient' risk assessment is the primary legal requirement. In addition, at least one person with a current paediatric first-aid certificate must accompany children on outings.

> *An assessment is a practical assessment of the benefits and the risks of the activity with a focus on hazards with the potential to cause real harm. It is not about creating a risk-free society, but about ensuring that reasonable precautions are taken to avoid injury.*
>
> Ball et al., 2009

Legally practitioners are required to carry out a 'suitable and sufficient' risk assessment of their provision and act on their findings. To acknowledge the children's need and desire for risk and challenge, while satisfying legal obligations, practitioners should evaluate the benefits alongside the potential risks. This benefit-risk assessment helps to decide what is reasonable and allows practitioners to consider other important factors such as the ages of the children, local circumstances and the use of natural features such as trees. It is important to note that equipment standards and other guidance are not mandatory.

Photo: Boldon Nursery Outdoor Nursery

Climbing trees is a traditional childhood activity often not permitted in the playground, but it has many benefits to the child including fun, gross motor development, self-esteem, problem solving, risk taking and general well-being.

There are no ratios specifically set for outings; meeting the same minimum ratios that apply at the service is mandatory. Our duty of care, benefit–risk assessments, policies and procedures should inform appropriate ratios and what is acceptable in the environment. Individual services may have their own policies and procedures. These are not mandatory and may be flexible after consultation and discussion with other practitioners.

With this knowledge, and the belief that such experiences are beneficial to children, a change in mind-set from 'We can't do that' to 'How can we do that?' is often witnessed.

Dangers beyond the fence

Fenced playgrounds are often considered safe, but experience has shown that there are far fewer serious injuries in wild nature. One reason could be that children are more alert and careful as it 'feels' more dangerous out there.

A young child is cautiously taking a risk in a space that 'feels' dangerous. He is extra careful – holding on tightly and accidents are therefore less likely to occur.

The table below shows the results of a survey of practitioners who have been taking children into wild nature, comparing the injuries sustained in the setting with those sustained in nature over the same time period. There are fewer accidents requiring medical treatment when children are in wild nature with its perception of higher risk.

Being away from a setting may mean that it is more difficult to get help in an emergency; this needs to be a consideration in policies, procedures and benefit-risk assessments.

Harm, hazards and risks

The words 'safe', 'harm', 'hazard' and 'risk' mean something different to different adults depending on their knowledge and level of risk averseness. There are cultural as well as individual differences in attitudes, interpretations and values placed on experiences we offer children. All should be equally considered when making a judgement about what is acceptable.

Harm and injury are emotive words. A common-sense approach is needed here. A paper cut is an injury; it is painful and takes time to heal but we would not consider removing paper from our lives. A serious physical injury has long-term permanent consequences whereas cuts, splinters, bruises, scrapes and, let's be radical, even a broken bone are common childhood injuries. Such injuries heal and should not be viewed as an excuse to rob children of adventurous and enjoyable childhood experiences.

Injuries within the setting	Injuries in wild nature
General first aid (plasters, hugs, cold compress etc.): 75%	General first aid (plasters, hugs, cold compress etc.): 15%
Actual medical attention (A&E, ambulance, stitches etc.): 1 - tripped up and hit head on step, needed butterfly stitches / steri-strips.	Actual medical attention (A&E, ambulance, stitches etc): 0.
Bumps and trips	None
	We have the odd scraped knee or bumped head but as a rule the children have a heightened sense of spatial awareness while in the outdoor space. They are confident and competent risk takers and assist each other if required.
On average 1 a year needing medical attention	None
Minimal	Minimal
Few scratches and stings	Had a few stings and scratches – nothing else.
Minimal	Minimal

Comparisons of injuries sustained in the licensed setting and wild nature over the same period.

Definitions

✿ Safe: the potential risks are acceptable, not that there is no risk of harm.

✿ Harm: an injury that has potential long-term physical or emotional consequences, not a graze, bruise, paper cut. Even a broken arm is not considered a serious injury; it too will heal.

✿ Hazard: something that has the potential to cause harm. In reality, everything has this potential. We focus on the learning and benefit of dealing with these to facilitate acceptable risk.

✿ Risk: means that the consequences and thus possible injury cannot be predicted. In risk assessments we weigh up the likelihood and severity of possible harm that such a risk could hold.

Children develop an awareness of others around them when playing with sticks at Dunblane Nature Kindergarten, an activity often discouraged in some traditional settings.

There is a tendency for 'catastrophic thinking' when considering children. This is an emotive subject, but always looking at worst-case scenarios is not helpful to adults or children. Here we explore the common-sense approach to risk taking, recognising the capability and benefits of children self-risk assessing and participating in risky play.

> *"Supposing a tree fell down, Pooh, when we were underneath it?" "Supposing it didn't!" said Pooh after careful thought. Piglet was comforted by this.*
>
> A. A. Milne

Adults dynamically assess risk as children explore to ensure they do not suffer serious avoidable injuries. This toddler at Nature Nurture is not prevented from touching this prickly leaf, allowing her to experience the feel of a holly leaf.

A PRACTICAL GUIDE TO Nature-Based Practice

Making a judgement

It is the role of the adult to assess possible hazards and risks and to then make an informed judgement on what is acceptable in the social context of children's play.

> *Good risks and hazards are acceptable and hold few surprises. Bad risks offer no obvious developmental or other benefits.*
>
> Ball et al., 2008

Some points to consider:

✿ The adult's role is to protect children from hazards where children may be unable to judge the severity of the potential risk. Hidden deep water would be an example and might need to be pointed out to children. Our role is not to protect children from hazards they can see and have the ability to judge for themselves. The ability to assess a hazard comes from knowledge and experience. Without this opportunity, children will struggle to self-risk assess appropriately.

✿ Children and adults lacking knowledge or experience may be unable to make informed judgements. This would apply to 'hidden' hazards such as dead wood in the tree canopy or a lack of knowledge about local toxic plants. Babies and toddlers, as well as some children with additional needs, may fall in this category due to lack of experience or opportunity.

✿ If risks are obvious, such as when climbing a tree or jumping from a height, this would be an acceptable hazard or as referred to above – a good hazard and risk. Fire is another such good hazard; even very young children know that fire is hot.

✿ If there are no obvious benefits and only risks, the hazard and experience would be avoided – a bad hazard and risk.

A 'good' risk is an obvious risk. This boy jumping over a small stream is not facing major hidden hazards, and his desire and sense of adventure is rewarded through overcoming the challenge he has set himself.

Visible hazards such as lighting a fire can be judged by the children as being risky and is therefore a good hazard; they tend to be very cautious.

Lack-of-freedom risk

One of the risks seldom considered is the harm adults may be causing children by restricting their freedom to play and explore. Research shows that this could have long-term permanent negative consequences for children and society.

Peter Gray (2014) has linked the decline of freedom to an increase in mental disorders; this is a serious risk with possible long-term consequences:

> *Over the past 60 years we have witnessed, in our culture, a continuous, gradual, but ultimately dramatic decline in children's opportunities to play freely, without adult control, and especially in their opportunities to play in risky ways. Over the same 60 years we have also witnessed a continuous, gradual, but ultimately dramatic increase in all sorts of childhood mental disorders, especially emotional disorders.*

Children are trying to tell us that they need excitement, that they need freedom and need to be trusted; we need to listen to them. Through such experiences they develop resilience and the ability to cope with what life throws at them.

The turbulent sea and height of the rocks are considered too dangerous to jump by this boy, who is experienced and trusted to self-risk assess the situation. The risks are obvious.

Emotional risk

Physical risks, such as scrapes, cuts and bruises are easily measurable and eventually heal. Emotional harm is less measurable but is more likely to have negative long-lasting or even permanent consequences. Lady Allen of Hurtwood is famously quoted:

> *It is better to risk a broken leg than a broken spirit. A leg can always mend. A spirit may not.*

I have watched the faces of young children change from exhilaration to despondency as they are yet again rebuked for their adventurous play. I have seen the doubt in a child's face when an adult overrides their confidence in their own abilities, telling them to get down or be careful. The risk of the emotional harm to children not trusted may have long-term permanent consequences.

Risk-taking dispositions

A risk-taking disposition means being prepared to have a go, to try something new and, if it doesn't work, to rethink and try again. Research shows that children who are risk takers outdoors are also likely to be risk takers indoors. Children take a social risk when attempting to join a group – the uncertainty of whether they would be accepted might prevent some from even trying.

In the classroom children prepared to have a go, to take a risk, will pick up a new book or try a difficult mathematics sum; they will be the first to try something new and not get stressed when it doesn't work. A risk-taking disposition is a positive trait and life skill encouraged and supported by nature-based practice.

> *Having a risk-taking disposition shows persistence in the face of difficulty and uncertainty. Persistence is seen as engaging with uncertainty, being prepared to be wrong, risking making a mistake and then going on to learn.*
>
> Carr, 1997

Having the ability to persevere at difficult tasks and having resilience are key factors in how well children adapt when they go to school and cope flexibly later in life.

Nature is unpredictable, and facing this uncertainty takes courage from both the practitioner and the child. Entering the unknown together as a group offers support as well as social risk. The sense of achievement at the end of such experiences is likely to encourage further explorations into uncertainty.

Climbing and playing together holds social, emotional as well as physical risks. It also offers adventure and challenge to these children at the Secret Garden Outdoor Nursery.

A baby investigating a pile of wet leaves, taking a risk as she might not know what this entails – she is embracing the unknown.

Balancing benefits and risks in children's play

Instead of only looking at opportunities with a negative attitude, it is important to look at what benefits may be offered, weighing up the benefits and the risks when making a judgment about whether an experience is worthwhile. If there are no benefits, the risk is not worth taking, while any benefits – and enjoyment counts as a benefit – may make the risk worth taking.

Children have a natural desire to seek out challenges and take risks; it is therefore important that such opportunities are available to satisfy this urge in a sensitively supervised environment. It is equally important that children become aware of hazards, are able to recognise risks to enable them to keep themselves safe.

NBP in action

TOOL USE

The use of appropriate woodworking tools in nature-based play is common, either at the centre or in wild nature. The benefits to children are numerous, including development of fine motor and gross motor development, self-esteem, organisational skills, independence and of course... fun and challenge.

These young children are developing their skill at using the junior hacksaw. Practitioners demonstrated safe use including the use of a glove on the hand not holding the saw. The first child attempted this and then discarded the glove; she needed the sensory input of bare hands to help her develop the manual dexterity to be able to use her saw. The second child had developed the skill of sawing and chose to wear gloves on both hands. He tried sawing and then removed the glove holding the saw, as he sensed that he had better control of his tool without the glove.

This more experienced boy on the Shetland Islands was eager to use the junior hacksaw to remove the bark off the stump. He was given the option of wearing a glove on his right hand after he was encouraged to identify the risk and possible consequences of the saw slipping. He made a choice not to wear the glove. The adult did a dynamic risk assessment and, using professional judgement, felt that any possible injury would be minor; the boy's perception was that he was handling a dangerous tool, leading to great caution.

When there is a perception of increased risk, children and adults are more aware of their surroundings and more cautious. Sometimes, creating a more obvious or bigger hazard increases children's awareness of the risks, thereby increasing caution and safety.

> One valuable approach to risk management in play provision is to make the risks as apparent as possible ... spaces where the risk of injury arises from hazards that children can readily appreciate such as heights.

Ball et al, 2008

When assessing risk, explore the reduction or adaptation of hazards to reduce possible risks, thereby allowing benefits to outweigh risks. Risk-reducing procedures reduce the severity or likelihood of the risk, thus enabling children to take part in worthwhile experiences. Be conscious of not removing all the identified benefits through unnecessary risk-reducing procedures.

Benefit-risk assessments

Outings should always be beneficial to the children. All outings need to be thoroughly planned and need to comply with your service or setting's outings policy documents, as well as health and safety requirements. Service policies are not regulations, so there may be an opportunity, after discussion, for flexibility within your organisation if policies and procedures are too restrictive and children are being deprived of valuable experiences. Considering and then documenting the benefits before contemplating the outing ensures that children have high-quality experiences.

Realising the benefits of an opportunity is vital and is identified before considering the risks. A benefit-risk assessment clearly considers the benefits, weighs this up against the possible risks and then puts in place procedures to reduce the risks without removing all the benefits.

To bring a balanced view as well as ownership to the process, the whole staff team and the children are consulted. Identified risk-reducing procedures have to be adhered to; they need to be logical, practical and achievable. It is advisable that all the adults sign to acknowledge that they have read, understood and agreed to follow the procedures identified.

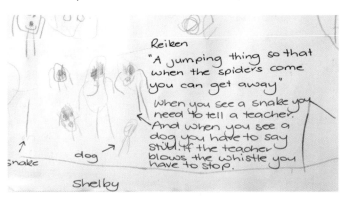

Children in this centre are able to keep themselves safe through knowing and understanding the agreed procedures to protect them from spiders, snakes and dogs.

Undertake an activity benefit–risk assessment for activities that could be perceived as being risky, such as tool use, tree climbing (see example on page 124), cooking on fire and working with ropes. The advantages are that:

✿ they can be referred to when doing an outing benefit–risk assessment to reduce paperwork.

✿ they raise adult awareness of the hazards, benefits and risks, as well as the procedures in place to reduce risk.

✿ they demonstrate to families that practitioners take their duty of care towards children seriously.

✿ when shared with parents these model the value of allowing children to take part in risky challenges.

✿ they provide support during regulatory visits.

Benefit-risk assessments are reviewed:

✿ annually

✿ if there are changes

✿ if there has been an incident

✿ when new relevant research becomes available

✿ when new relevant information is received.

Dynamic benefit-risk assessments

There are times when predicting every eventuality is not possible, and this is where dynamic benefit-risk assessments come in. How can we know what children will do, and how can we write risk assessments on everything? In short, we can't – not in advance, not in writing. It is for the providers to use their professional judgement on whether the risk assessment needs to be in writing.

Children and the environment may not always behave in the expected manner; benefit-risk assessments may not correctly predict the risks. This is where an alert and skilled practitioner is able to make an on-the-spot judgement: a dynamic benefit-risk assessment.

The natural environment is constantly changing, seasonally as well as through the fauna and flora. Having such variables means that adults and children need to be skilled at dynamic benefit–risk assessments. Essentially, this kind of assessment relies on being able to make judgements on the here and now without necessarily stopping play or having paper documentation.

Dynamic benefit–risk assessments support children's uninterrupted flow in play while at the same time ensuring children are as safe as necessary:

> *Dynamic benefit–risk assessments are the minute-by-minute observations and potential interventions by adults with a sound grasp of how children learn and grow through play. It is by its nature, complex and fluid. This form of assessment is not readily documented and is often undervalued because there may not be written evidence that procedures are being followed.*
>
> Ball et al., 2008

A transparent jellyfish found in the sea 'needs' to be investigated immediately by the child; the adult does a quick on-the-spot dynamic benefit-risk assessment, makes a professional judgement and then supports the exploration.

A community of risk assessors

Adults and children all have different views and personal limitations on acceptable risk, often formed from previous memories and past experiences which can affect our ability to make balanced decisions. For example, having a fear of heights might affect an adult's ability to make a sound judgment about children climbing trees.

Decisions on what constitutes acceptable risk should be made by the practitioners and children in consultation with families. Having said that, one concerned parent's view should not jeopardise valuable experiences for a group of children; neither should we benchmark down at the level of the most anxious practitioner either, as we discussed in chapter 4.

> *If you want to allow all children the chance to spread their wings a little, you cannot set your bar at the level of the most anxious parent.*
>
> Gill, 2012

Children as risk assessors and risk takers

Young children instinctively know what they need for their development, and testing their limits is important to them. They will seek out such opportunities, and if the environment does not offer this, they will create their own challenges which may not be appropriate and in fact, may be far more dangerous. For example, children who have access only to developmentally inappropriate climbing opportunities will climb the drainpipes or the fences to satisfy this need, and practitioners may find themselves constantly telling children to stop climbing.

> *Children need the freedom to take risks in play because it allows them to continually test the limits of their physical, intellectual and emotional development.*
>
> Tranter 2005

Children learn about their own courage physically and emotionally as they push themselves right to the edge of THEIR comfort zone (often well beyond the comfort zone of some adults!) and then develop resilience as they extend their comfort zone.

If we don't test our limits, how do we know what our limits are? How do we establish new limits? Extending that comfort zone is what it is about. How high, how low, how far, how fast, how slow, how many, how few... Challenge includes an element of risk – emotional, social and/or physical.

Trusting children to be capable risk takers allows them the freedom to challenge themselves by climbing onto the roof of the wooden house to 'paint' it at Dunblane Nature Kindergarten. Only one boy felt the need to achieve this; others felt the same level of risk by standing on the low bench.

Intuitive self-risk assessing

Every child is different. Some are considered dare-devils or adrenaline junkies, constantly looking for challenge and risk, while others are cautious. It is as if each child has their own risk threshold.

Very young children use their instinct and intuition – that knowledge that sits deep within us that something is just not right. This is a very personal emotion. Some babies will happily approach one adult but shy away from another. Some will be fearful of the waves on the beach while others are fascinated. It can seem that many children appear to have lost that ability to 'listen' to their instinct: could this be because others do the risk assessing for them and they have been taught to obey? Children need to be able to 'feel' that instinct, that intuition to know when things don't feel right. That is the way they are able to keep themselves safe when adults are not around.

One child will confidently leap off a rock while others observe. Some will attempt to jump from a lower height, each child jumping from a height they feel comfortable with and each feeling a similar sense of achievement.

Risky play

Practitioners may feel that they are constantly telling children to 'be careful', 'don't climb', 'stop running', 'come out of there' and 'stop fighting'. Sandseter (2011) observed children on playgrounds in Norway, England and Australia and identified six categories of risky play:

✿ exploring heights such as climbing a wall, a tree or a den, swinging very high.

✿ experiencing high speed such as running, swinging or cycling fast.

✿ being near dangerous elements such as fire or water.

✿ rough-and-tumble play which boys in particular participate in when they are 'wrestling' with each other.

✿ wandering alone away from adult supervision. The child may wander off around the corner – usually first making sure that the adult knows they are going.

✿ handling dangerous tools such as a real knife and fork, a pocket knife, a fire steel, real gardening tools, a saw and hand drill.

These forms of risky play will be very familiar, recognised as behaviours often discouraged in settings. These instinctive risky play behaviours are supported in nature-based practice.

Many playgrounds are developed so that children are unable to take part in such risky play or have limited opportunities. In wild nature there is a perception of increased risk by both the children and the adults. Adults appear to accept this as a space in which they have less control over the environment, while the obviously risk-rich natural environment encourages children to explore with joy and sensible caution.

> " We deprive children of free, risky play, ostensibly to protect them from danger, but in the process we set them up for mental breakdowns. Children are designed by nature to teach themselves emotional resilience by playing in risky, emotion-inducing ways. In the long run, we endanger them far more by preventing such play than by allowing it. And, we deprive them of fun.
>
> Gray, 2014 "

When children are left to manage themselves without adult interference there are less likely to be tears. It is often when adults urge them to 'be careful' or 'help' them in activities the children are not confident in, that incidents may happen.

> " Play, to be safe, must be free play, not coerced, managed, or pushed by adults.
>
> Gray 2014 "

Photo: Clare Nugent

Using real tools satisfies a desire and need for risky play. This boy has made the choice not to wear a protective glove while using the bowsaw; he is very aware of the possible risks and has consciously placed the saw away from the hand holding the branch. This heightened awareness and additional risk is what he desired.

A supporting adult finger at Into the Woods Outdoor Nursery. A moment's hesitation to assess the risks for herself before she makes the decision to continue.

Children of all ages tend to be drawn to water where there is a perception of increased danger – one of the risky play behaviours supported at River Cottage Nursery.

At Nature Nurture a child helps to collect and carry water from the stream to the fire circle as part of the risk assessment process.

Modelling the risk-assessment process

Children's contribution and involvement should be sought when developing procedures to reduce risks to an acceptable level. Through this, we model the risk-assessment process raising awareness of possible hazards and risks. Children will then know and understand why procedures have been put in place and not feel that adults are just out to spoil their fun.

NBP in action

KEEPING SAFE

These children had a very good knowledge of the possible hazards as well as the risks involved in using these tools when asked by the adults: 'How do we keep safe with tools?'

Caitlyn: 'We don't leave them lying around or people will trip over them.'

Imogen: 'You don't put your hands near the tools.'

Mia knew how to use the whittler safely: 'Scrape away from your fingers.'

Lucy was concerned about the fire steel: 'Don't do the firelighter in someone's face.'

They were offered the opportunity to reflect on their experiences.

Mia, after cutting her finger with the saw: 'Don't cut yourself like I did. I should have put a glove on.'

When accidents occur

Accidents may happen; in fact accidents will happen. It is a normal part of childhood and should be viewed as such; these are 'learning injuries'. The vast majority of accidents are easily sorted with a hug and a plaster; occasionally medical treatment may be required. After a serious accident, it is important that all have the time to recover, reflect and gain some perspective.

Ball, Gill & Spiegal (2008) stated that while it is acceptable that during play children may be at risk of minor or easily-healed injuries, children should not be exposed to a significant likelihood of permanent disability or life-threatening injuries. At times it may be unavoidable that during play children are exposed to a very low risk of serious injury or death. They stated that this would only be tolerable in the following conditions:

> ◆ 'the likelihood was extremely low
>
> ◆ the hazards were clear to users
>
> ◆ there were obvious benefits
>
> ◆ further reduction of the risk would remove the benefits
>
> ◆ there were no reasonably practical ways to manage the risk'.

Having a knowledge of possible hazards

Identifying possible hazards and risks allows appropriate hazard reduction procedures. If hypothermia or heatstroke is a risk, there needs to be a sound knowledge of the symptoms. If snakes, rats or ticks are a risk, there needs to be the knowledge to deal with them and the possible consequences.

It is important that the most up-to-date information is gathered for your unique situation. This is the responsibility of the practitioner undertaking the risk assessment.

Just as important is that children encounter hazards such as spiders, fungi, berries etc. in an adult-supervised space so that these encounters can be used to increase children's knowledge, thereby allowing them to keep themselves safe.

Fungi are fascinating; keep children safe by raising awareness of the possibility of some fungi being poisonous and therefore the need for a hand-washing procedure after handling such possible hazardous material.

Extremes in temperature

Children are very sensitive to high and low temperatures and can become distressed very quickly. Be aware of the weather and realise that children can quickly lose body heat when they are cold; consider the dampness of snow and the possible wind chill factor in an exposed area. Ensure children have access to shelter, dry clothing and warmth and know how to identify and treat hypothermia. Although less common in the UK, know how to identify and treat heat stress, heat exhaustion and heat stroke symptoms.

Wildlife

Most of the fauna in the UK is relatively harmless and only concerned with going about their own business. Here we focus on some of those considered more dangerous and most likely to be encountered.

Taught knowledge, experience and skill enables these children to keep safe while exploring dead jellyfish found on the beach.

Snakes

Snakes are not often encountered in the UK but they are there. Practitioners should inform children on how they can keep safe by not trapping or stepping onto a snake.

Information from the Forestry Commission on snakes is that 'the adder is the only venomous snake native to Britain. Adders have the most highly-developed venom-injecting mechanism of all snakes, but they are not aggressive animals. Adders will only use their venom as a last means of defence, usually if caught or trodden on.'

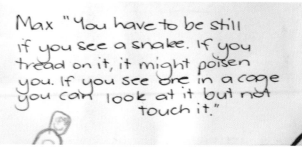

Max "You have to be still if you see a snake. If you tread on it, it might poisen you. If you see one in a cage you can look at it but not touch it."

A child shares his knowledge on what to do should they encounter a snake.

Spiders

There is no record of anyone dying from a spider bite in Britain — occasionally one may give a nasty nip. Spiders and their webs are regularly removed from the children's environment as part of a maintenance routine. But how will curious children learn to keep safe from these fascinating creatures if they don't see and learn about them and their intricate webs? Spiders in general evoke fear and even phobias, but here is some reassuring information. Again, it is important to do your own research.

> *The fact is that, from a human perspective, spiders just aren't that dangerous. While many spiders can give you a nip, in most cases it is less troublesome than a bee sting.*
>
> Dr Aaron Harmer, arachnid researcher, Macquarie University

Photo by Kyle Champness

Getting to know spiders in your environment is important. Children in New Zealand are more likely to be familiar with spiders as there are no poisonous spiders there. In Australia, children are generally taught to fear and avoid spiders and consequently tend to have less knowledge.

NBP in action

VALUING WILDLIFE AS A LEARNING OPPORTUNITY

A young boy creating a spider's web structure in a 'forest' on the Shetland Islands noticed a small spider climbing along the wool. Initially concerned as he has a fear of spiders, he called to the adult who identified the spider as harmless and encouraged him to use his camera to explore the spider more closely. He then had the confidence to move close to the spider to take a photograph.

Reflection:

Adults did a dynamic benefit–risk assessment and encouraged this boy and the other children to investigate closely. Children realised that not all spiders are dangerous. There was a sharing of knowledge between the adult and the children.

By taking photographs of the spider and the web this experience can be extended within the setting and at home, exploring spiders in depth, looking at safety, habitats, food, camouflage, webs and so much more. A contextual learning opportunity.

Ticks

Ticks can transmit bacteria that cause diseases such as Lyme disease. Although not all tick bites result in disease, it is important you know how to avoid tick bites and to take action if you get bitten. They are usually found in woodlands, grassland, moorland, heathland and some urban parks and gardens throughout the UK.

> *Symptoms of Lyme disease can include flu-like symptoms, fatigue, muscle and joint pain. A characteristic expanding rash, erythema migrans, is present in most but not all cases. Lyme disease can be treated with a course of antibiotics but prevention and early detection are crucial.*
>
> PHE Ticks and Your Health 2016

General guidelines when walking in areas where ticks may occur include:

- wear light-coloured clothing to cover arms and legs and tuck trousers into socks
- brush clothing down before coming inside
- check neck and scalp as well as other warm, moist areas
- know what to do if you find a tick lodged in your skin and how best to remove it
- know how to manage allergic reactions to tick bites, including anaphylaxis
- consider using an insect repellent.

> *Current advice on tick removal is to remove it as soon as possible, use a pair of fine-tipped tweezers, or a tick removal tool, grasp as close to the skin as possible, pull upwards slowly and firmly as mouthparts left in the skin can cause a local infection. Don't use petroleum jelly, alcohol, a lit match or any other method to try to remove a tick. Once removed apply antiseptic to the bite area, or wash with soap and water and keep an eye on it for several weeks for any changes and contact the GP if you begin to feel unwell.*
>
> PHE Ticks and Your Health 2016

The Australian Society of Clinical Immunology and Allergy recommends against removing a living tick – killing the tick with an ether-containing spray such as 'Wart-Off' before removal to prevent an allergic reaction.

It is important that practitioners regularly research up-to-date information on best practice.

Foxes

Foxes do often come into contact with humans and attacks have occurred, although this is very rare.

Jellyfish

Virtually all jellyfish can sting, and several are considered native to the UK. One, (although not actually a jellyfish) is a common summer visitor: the Portuguese Man o' War (Physalia physalis). It's sting may cause unpleasant symptoms but there have been no recorded deaths in the UK.

Wasps and bees

These are considered the most dangerous 'animals' in the UK, killing about five people annually due to an allergic reaction to the venom.

There is so much more I could say about risk and the benefit of risk but the most important message I have is that the only way we can keep children safe is by them being able to keep themselves safe. Adults cannot always be with children to protect them – they need to share their knowledge with the children. Children need this knowledge and experience to be able to keep themselves safe; that is the only way they can be safe.

Chapter 6

Natural creativity

> *It is in playing and only in playing that the individual child or adult is able to be creative and to use the whole personality, and it is only in being creative that the individual discovers the self.*
>
> Donald Winnicott

Nature-based practice encourages natural creativity in its broadest holistic sense to include art, construction, cooking, role play, music, stories and so much more.

A child given the time, freedom and support by adults who appreciate and support the child's self-initiated experiences will develop the security and desire to play imaginatively. Children will feel they belong, have ownership and will work together effectively, communicating with each other on multiple levels.

> *Children's play in natural environments contains more imaginative and creative components that foster language and collaborative skills.*
>
> Fjortoft & Sageie, 2000

What do children actually do when they are in a natural environment? In this chapter we will explore some of the play and learning practitioners might observe in a nature-based setting. Without adult-designed, pre-manufactured toys in the space, and without adult direction, children are driven to explore, push their boundaries and use the natural found resources in multiple ways. This leads to high levels of imaginative and creative play.

Two children created a fairy garden with a swimming pool in a shell, floating flower for fairies to rest and enjoy the sun on, and a slide made of a razor shell. They worked together cooperatively, building on each other's creative ideas.

Creative play

Authentic natural creativity comes from long periods of uninterrupted time in a natural space full of opportunities. Some children may initially feel or look bored; this may have negative connotations both in perceptions and in the knowledge that this child has momentarily lost the ability to appreciate the freedom offered and is waiting for instructions. Such 'unfilled' time is often necessary to encourage the creative thinking process and does not need to be 'filled' by a well-meaning adult.

Sticks have a very high play appeal and affordance for children of all ages, naturally lending themselves to creative thinking. A weapon, gate, writing tool, wand or barrier. These children at Brae Primary School on the Shetland Islands demonstrated high-level skills and knowledge of engineering, technology, science and maths concepts.

Found resources

The number and variety of materials found in nature offers a huge self-select 'pick and mix' of natural materials unique to each space. Open-ended resources with multiple uses, resources that are influenced by the seasons, constantly changing, often decomposing into new forms. Leaves may be green and pliable, come in beautiful shades of red, or brown, curled up, crunchy and brittle – each stage offering its own unique creative and learning experiences.

One certainty is that there is uncertainty – children never know what they will find – it is often in this unpredictability and subtle detail that children are motivated to think and explore creatively.

> *... the constantly-evolving natural world creates an infinite number of variables for children to interact with.*
>
> Nicholson, 1971

Leaves are just leaves to most adults, but to one child they provided a collecting, sorting and matching opportunity as she carefully arranged them along the bench.

Transient art

Nature art work is transient – it is not glued down; it changes, often affected by time or weather. Some of the staples of indoor art are not needed – no paint, no paper, no glue and no glitter. These have a use in an indoor environment, but outdoors we look for a different experience and not a replication of the indoor opportunities. This practice is sustainable as natural materials can be reused and absorbed back into nature.

Children will carefully select and place the materials, and what may often appear random to adults is actually very deliberate thinking. They might balance stones or sticks, or mould sand and soil into 3D structures using only their hands, developing muscle control. Mini and full-size functional structures include fairy houses, mini bridges, dens to play in, and sandcastles decorated with shells and seaweed.

Children take ownership and change their environment. They do not need to pack away; they delight in finding evidence of their previous play while wondering about the changes that may have occurred.

This garden for fairies evolved over time with different children collaborating and adding individual touches with found items that inspired them.

Children (and adults) of all ages will gather and place stones in water, often stacking them into piles or balancing them in towers of increasing complexity.

Mud is a sensorial mixture that motivates children to explore using all their senses. Making mixtures playfully develops scientific and mathematical concepts.

A sandcastle built and decorated with natural materials is reclaimed by the incoming tide, only to be rebuilt another day, a natural cycle.

Natural encounters fuel children's creativity; objects have no preset function – they can be anything and everything the child desires. They may take this knowledge back to the setting and choose to work differently with their new-found knowledge and creativity.

NBP in action

A TRANSIENT ART GALLERY

Andy Goldsworthy is famous for his transient art using natural materials. Photographs of his work were offered as inspiration to the children at Forrest After School Club in Australia which inspired them to create their own art gallery using the natural material found in their playground. After a stormy night, things had changed; lighter objects had been added or blown away by the wind, providing a contextual scientific learning experience. Children could now choose to repair, change or observe further changes over time.

Mark making

Children from a very young age are driven to make marks which help to develop gross and fine motor control and communication skills. This exploration progresses to decorating, drawing and symbolic writing.

Nature offers many wonderful, rich mark-making materials. Sticks, shells and leaves can be used to mark a pathway with arrows, symbols and letters. Soil, sand, and natural clay mixed with water makes natural paints. Flowers, leaves, fungi and lichen can be crushed to create colour. Charcoal after a campfire can be used dry or as a paint when water is added. A finger, feather or stick can be used as a mark-making tool when dipped into a puddle of water. Using this on a hot dry stone and watching the marks disappear in the heat raises questions about scientific concepts such as evaporation.

Mark making can also take the form of scratching using fingers, a stick or a shell to scratch shapes, letters or numbers in the sand, soil or snow. Carving would require a harder 'tool' (shell, stick, stone, metal, knife) to cut into a softer material such as a piece of bark, soft wood, seed pod or pumice stone.

Scratching and carving a name using a hard implement or creating a pattern on a bow with a penknife indicate ownership and a sense of identity.

NBP in action

MAKING ROCK PAINT

Discovering that some rocks can be 'dissolved' and crushed is often the start of an intensive period of creative scientific investigation. Rocks are not all equal; a harder stone can scratch into or break up a softer stone. A nine year old boy in Scotland discovered scratching a hard stick along a wet stone produced colour and he used this technique to write on his arm. He explored further, searching for softer stones, finding one that could be crushed with a hard stone to make a powder. Adding water, he discovered making paint out of rocks that could be used to make marks on leaves and sticks.

Imaginative play

Wild nature lends itself to highly-imaginative play. Children can move freely and have a myriad of natural resources to transform into anything and everything. The same piece of wood can be a mobile phone, a ticket or a sandwich; the fallen tree can be a seat, space rocket, ice-cream shop, horse or dinosaur.

A leaf started off as a green hand, then transformed into a plate on which to serve an assortment of natural (inedible) delicacies.

This multi-functionality of natural materials supports transformational play, engaging children for long periods of time and allowing play to continuously change without a break in flow. Children don't stop to argue about a toy or a space, they don't stop to tidy up – they play until they are finished or are ready to leave and come back later.

Storytelling

Adults often need the security offered by a story book rather than freely telling a story. Telling rather than reading a story allows the storyteller to make eye contact with the audience and actively engage them in the imaginative process. Telling a story about a found object comes naturally to children: a bone becomes a dinosaur bone; a pine cone becomes a fairy house, each with a highly-imaginative story behind it.

Creating story sticks or story stones promotes imaginative as well as functional story telling with appeal to different children, allowing all children to be storytellers.

Children at Darvell School, motivated by the Stick Man book, searched for a variety of sticks to shape their own Stick Men, which are now found all over the school in a range of poses and sizes.

Sticks broken into similar lengths to create a small world bridge exploring and developing science, technology, engineering and mathematics concepts. Stories about the Billy Goats Gruff were shared, re-enacted and adapted by the children.

A fairy house which evolved over a whole day with different children contributing carpets, beds, gardens, camouflage, chandeliers, a toilet and a dog as part of an ongoing story! Being able to build a 3D structure requires skills which tend to be passed on from one group of children to another, or by the adult modelling this alongside the children.

Role play

Role play is a feature of nature-based play; imaginative children without access to adult-designed, pre-manufactured resources or toys will use natural materials to symbolise the necessary props. This ability to use the concept of symbols in play supports progression to symbols such as letters and numbers.

A rock-grinding factory. In this setting the white stones were hard to find, so children gave them a higher value than the other stones.

A stone becomes the symbol for a mobile phone, with children mimicking the actions and tone of voice heard. Children tend to use a piece of bark or a stick, but in the Shetland Islands these can be hard to find; this little girl had the same intent, used the same actions with the material available to her.

Objects hidden in a tree hollow indicate a treasure – materials of value to the individual child or group of children.

Large outdoor spaces support large 'stages', inviting children to use their imagination, to change scenes frequently without interruption to their play. A 'dragon' tree can be slain by the brave who descend with their stick weapons before moving on to the hot chocolate shop on the big rock to feed the cold warriors, before they join the others jumping off a 'diving board' and into the muddy puddle next to the sycamore tree. This sort of extended role play is not often available indoors.

Many children enjoy playing shop as they have direct experience of shopping. Children often establish a currency depending on the perceived value and scarcity of an object. In an environment where there are no sticks, the sticks would have a high trading 'value'; the sticks in the tree hollow are in the 'safe'. The white stones in the 'shop' have the highest currency value. Children collect the stones, bring them to the 'grinding/smashing' place and are paid in powdered stone, in effect bartering and establishing 'shops'. Interestingly these traditional role play games are passed on from year to year, often through generations.

Secret spaces give a perception of solitude where children can be imaginative in their thinking and creating.

THE CLAY WAND SHOP

Children at Redlands Kindergarten in Australia discovered a supply of natural clay. A young boy used his hands to mould even-sized balls and placed them on a small square plank. He pushed a stick into each ball: 'I am making wands'.

Together, he and the other children created their shop, writing 'The wand shop' using a piece of charcoal and then they were open for business. This extended constructive role play evolved during the session. There were no initial plans or programmes developed by the children or the adults; it just happened. Such imaginative role play has numerous learning and developmental opportunities that can be shared with families.

Using his hands to scrape and shape the balls

Manipulating the clay into even-sized shapes

One-to-one correspondence with a stick for each sphere

The wand shop – open for business

Music and sounds

Nature IS music. Apparent silence has gentle sounds – buzzing insects, flying birds, moving leaves and lapping water. Many children and adults living in a world dominated by constant noise no longer hear these subtle sounds of nature.

Nature-based practice encourages soft voices by adults and children – the space also belongs to the birds and animals. Initially adults may need to point out the bird song, but as children's hearing adapts they will pick up the quiet sounds. They might copy these sounds using their voices and natural materials – tapping sea shells, shaking seaweed, rustling leaves and dripping water.

Children will naturally pick up a stick and knock it against a tree or a rock. Tap and listen to the sound. Do all trees sound the same? Tap stones, shells, sticks, seedpods together – create a nature band.

Building a small shelter, the little girl created a pathway of stones leading up to it. She realised that tapping on the stones created different sounds and quietly shared that: 'These are music stones' while playing a range of 'tunes'.

Modelling creative skills

Some skills can be modelled or taught by the practitioner, who then moves back, allowing children to further develop their skills. For example:

- ✿ Join leaves together using small sticks.
- ✿ Thread leaves onto a stick.
- ✿ Thread shells onto dried seaweed or grass.
- ✿ Connect stalks of the leaves.
- ✿ Lash objects together using grass, seaweed or reed.
- ✿ Join daisies in a chain.
- ✿ Whistle using an acorn cup, shell or grass.
- ✿ Carve or 'drill' into pumice stone with a stick or shell.

The adult demonstrated how the stalk of the leaf could create a curved 'boat'. Children created a fleet of leaf yachts to race in a small stream after an adult modelled pushing the stalk of the leaf back into the leaf.

Using small sticks and 'stitching' leaves together is a skill children master quickly and will then use to create many articles, both functional and artistic. The young girl linked three oak leaves as a sail for a boat she made out of a piece of wood and decorated with charcoal out of the fire.

A leaf container made by 'stitching' four leaves together with small sticks.

There are many traditional skills using natural materials that may be demonstrated to even very young children. Using reed to create baskets by removing the pith of the reed, stripping it into thin strips, before twisting and weaving some of these through the upright strands was demonstrated by this dexterous five-year-old girl.

Cooking creatively

Cooking is not often valued as a creative opportunity, but being outdoors often requires adaptation and creative thinking. There is nothing as rewarding and exciting as cooking your own food on a fire you have helped create. The obvious would be to find food in the forest or catch your own fish, but this is not always a practical option. Being able to forage for your own food in nature is rewarding and free, but is a skill that is often taught by an experienced person.

Let's get cooking

Cooking is a highlight for many children (and adults) and deciding what to eat may take some negotiation. Healthy eating policies have a place, but a common sense approach is advised. When children have been outside, actively busy, a marshmallow or hot chocolate on a cold day while sitting around the fire is sociable and creates a sense of 'tribe'.

Considerations:

✿ Complete a 'cooking on fire' benefit–risk assessment.

✿ Meat, fish and perishable foods might not be appropriate unless approved transporting and storage facilities are available.

✿ Be aware of children with allergies or sensitivities and replace ingredients where appropriate.

Appropriate resources: a lidded Dutch oven to bake or boil food in and a ceramic fire bowl big enough for a small fire to cook marshmallows on.

Cooking on a stick

Nothing beats being in control of your food while it is cooking! Children select a green stick with the appropriate diameter and length for the purpose, whittle the stick into a point using a whittler (vegetable peeler) or a short-bladed knife to remove the bark and 'spike' the food. Rotate above the embers; children will learn through experience that the best way to cook is over embers, rather than flames. ENJOY!

Cooking sliced or small whole apples on sticks is a healthy option. Dip apples in brown sugar and children will enjoy caramelised apple.

Children make their own choices, cooking a marshmallow on a very short stick; experiencing the heat of the fire and possibly choosing a longer stick is part of the experiential learning.

Often it is the process that is the appeal, rather than the desire for a cooked marshmallow. Some children like their marshmallows well done or burnt black. Support young children in counting to ten before touching the hot food, allowing it to cool down enough not to cause a burn.

Food to cook on a stick:

❀ marshmallows: cook the marshmallow until soft; squash between two chocolate digestive biscuits with chocolate facing inwards – known as 'S'mores'.

❀ whole small apples.

❀ slices of apple or carrot dipped in cinnamon and brown sugar.

❀ slices of vegetable: courgette, carrot, peppers, mushroom, thin potato.

❀ whole egg: make a small hole (diameter of the stick) on one end of the egg, push the stick through carefully to the other end, make another small hole there so that the stick fits snuggly through the whole egg. Rotate over the fire.

❀ stick bread: mix self-rising flour with savoury ingredients (salt, herbs, cheese) or sweet ingredients (sugar, cinnamon, raisins, fruit) and add enough water to give a non-sticking dough. Children shape this around a bamboo or stick that has been soaked in water to prevent it burning. The thinner the dough around the stick, the better; otherwise they may be eating semi-raw dough (not a problem either). Hold over the fire and rotate to cook evenly.

Water-soaked bamboo stick bread rotated over the flames while banana surprise parcels are placed into the embers. This raisin bread is unlikely to cook through – children learn to add less dough or spread it more thinly for it to cook through evenly.

Surprise parcels

A sheet of aluminium foil wrapped and sealed to create a parcel can be filled with ingredients to be steamed in their own juices or a little water, stock, butter or oil. Every child could make their own and ingredients could include:

❀ mixed hard vegetables (potatoes, sweet potatoes, onions).

❀ mixed soft vegetables (courgette, mushrooms, peppers, eggplant).

❀ fruit (apples with raisins, plums, pineapple).

❀ fish cut into small pieces.

❀ thinly-sliced meat and vegetables.

❀ whole potatoes wrapped and placed in the coals.

❀ banana split surprise: whole banana in the skin, cut a slit along the inside curved length and fill with marshmallows, chocolate, raisins, nuts. Some prefer these wrapped in foil, otherwise the banana can be placed straight into the fire with the skin protecting.

❀ apple caramel surprise: whole apple, core removed and filled with raisins, sugar and butter, wrapped in foil and placed in the embers.

❀ popcorn – place two tablespoons of corn and two tablespoons of oil into the centre of a large piece of foil, fold the corners/ edges together leaving plenty of air space, tie to a green stick with a piece of twine and dangle above the fire, wait for the popping to stop – enjoy!

Boiling in a tin can

Boiling your own food in your own tin can is an exciting adventure. Use a clean can with label removed, put the choice of foods with water into the can and place into the fire. BEWARE – the can will be hot. Younger children will need adult help. Parents have commented that a child who usually refuses to eat boiled potatoes will eat them when cooked in their own tin can. You could cook:

❀ a small potato, carrot, broccoli, corn

❀ fruit

❀ soup

❀ stew

❀ noodles.

Boiling water

Hot chocolate or a cup of tea on a cold day can be quickly made by boiling water in a metal kettle on the fire or, even better, by using a Kelly Kettle. Collect kindling and light a small fire in the base, place the kettle filled with water onto the base, add more kindling through the central hole and, within minutes, the water is boiling. Try nettle or mint tea with the children. The Kelly Kettle also works in wet and windy conditions making it ideal for warming up on those regular cold days. Risk awareness tip - younger children tend to want to see the sticks and flames inside the central hole, not realising that the hole acts as a chimney for heat.

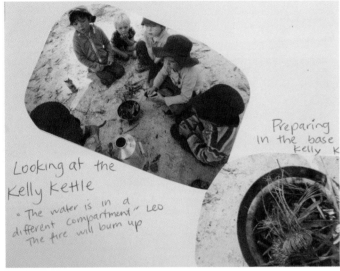

Looking at the Kelly Kettle

"The water is in a different compartment" Leo
The fire will burn up

Preparing in the base Kelly K

'The water is in a different compartment...the fire will burn up' commented a four-year-old, explaining his understanding of how the Kelly Kettle works. The technology and science behind this 'gadget' interests children and can be further extended.

Popcorn cooked in two strainers allows children to really experience and explore the science behind corn popping

After shaping a long-handled 'pan' using aluminium foil, melt a piece of chocolate over the fire, dip a marshmallows or biscuit into the warm chocolate and ENJOY.

Even more creative cooking

Be creative – adapt favourite recipes to enable a similar experience around the fire, and if it doesn't work, try another way. It is important to share success as well as failure with the children. Small frying pans, muffin pans and tins will work well, or create small individual cooking pots or spoons using aluminium foil.

- ❀ Popcorn: use two large metal strainers (pop out any plastic handle) and tie the metal handles to a long stick. Add corn to one strainer, close with the other to form a rounded lid (use a metal hook) and hold over the fire – WATCH and hear the corn pop. Even small individual metal tea strainers work, popping one or two corn kernels.

- ❀ Pancakes: use a small frying pan, extend the handle with a longer stick or make a mini, long-handled frying pan out of aluminium foil. Add a little butter and pour in the dough.

- ❀ Cheese or chocolate: using a sturdy stick attach aluminium foil to one end and shape into a spoon or bowl, add chocolate or cheese, hold above the embers to melt.

- ❀ Fondue: individual tea light fondues are great fun and create a sense of ownership. Use a small empty tin can (label removed) large enough to hold a tea light candle. Light using a flaming stick. Use a nail to make air holes in the sides of the tin. Shape an aluminium foil 'bowl' to hang above the candle. Place a square of chocolate or cheese in the bowl; when melted, dip in a mini marshmallow, biscuit, fruit, bread on a small stick.

- ❀ Dipping soup: create a tea-light pot as above and add some clear soup or stock into the bowl. Dip bread cubes.

- ❀ Orange cakes: cut oranges in half, squeeze the juice out and then remove the pith. Mix a simple cake mix or use a packet mix and pour into the orange halves, place in the fire and cook until ready.

- ❀ Bacon and eggs: place rashers of bacon into muffin pans forming little bowls. Cook until ready, then break an egg into each and return to the embers.

Fondue for one or two with children in control. Chocolate, cheese or soup stock can be used to dip into. Although the can does get moderately hot, the heat is unlikely to cause any serious burns unless children lack the impulse to feel and withdraw from the heat. This is very much about the process rather than the end product, and children are unlikely to eat enough to replace a meal.

Cooking using solar power

During hot summer days, children enjoy the process of creating a pizza box oven. This is not suitable for cooking meat or foods that need a minimum safe temperature to cook. The pizza box solar cooker reaches temperatures of about 100°C on a hot sunny day while the temperature of a candle flame is about 1000°C.

To make the oven:

✿ Cut a flap in the lid of a pizza box by making cuts about two to three cm from three of the edges.

✿ Fold the flap out so that it stands up when the box is closed. (image 1)

✿ Cover the inner side of the flap with aluminium foil, smoothing this out to create a reflector panel.

✿ Open the box and create an airtight window over the flap opening by taping a double layer of plastic wrap over the hole.

✿ Line the bottom of the box with smooth aluminium foil to reflect the heat.

✿ Place a square of black construction paper onto the bottom foil leaving a 2 cm border of foil. Black absorbs heat. (image 2)

✿ Place the oven in a sunny spot, adjust the reflector flap until as much sunlight as possible is reflected onto the plastic window. Use a stick to prop the flap at the right angle.

✿ After about 30 minutes, place food onto the black paper, close the oven, position reflector again and watch it heat. (image 3)

How does it work? The solar box oven converts sunlight to heat energy and retains the heat for cooking. As the heat is retained, the air inside the oven also heats up and the food cooks.

Some foods to cook in a solar oven:

✿ sprinkle cheese on a slice of bread with tomato sauce/Marmite to make mini pizzas

✿ thin slices of fruit and vegetables

✿ melting chocolate and marshmallows

✿ small thin pieces of dough to make mini biscuits

✿ reheating foods that do not contain meat and do not need to be reheated to a set temperature.

Pretend stew on a real fire

To young children the science of cooking is fascinating, to take raw ingredients like flour and water and magically create bread. As scientists they will want to explore this concept in a variety of opportunities.

Children at Child First, Northampton, wanted to make a special 'stew' and collected 'ingredients' such as sticks, leaves, soil and even a found sock! These were added to a large pot and placed onto the fire. Waiting for the 'stew' to cook is a time to be together, to watch, communicate, enjoy the sensorial environment and then to delight in the results.

These are just some of the suggestions for nature-based creative opportunities to get you started. The possibilities are endless; traditional skills such as weaving, felting, basketry, woodworking and papermaking are further opportunities to explore within your setting. Give them a go. Be adventurous, be brave and be creative, and if it doesn't work then simply try again in a different way!

Considerations for nature-based practice

Clare Nugent & Sarah MacQuarrie

A note from Niki:

In this last chapter two great friends, colleagues and academic researchers have shared further research-based information on the considerations for nature-based practice. They share with you the key components of nature-based practice; no two settings will be the same but there are a number of concepts that are consistent. They encourage you to think about what nature-based practice can look like for you, using your expert knowledge and experience of your location, environment and situation.

What has nature-based practice come to mean?

The answer to this question will vary for different practitioners in different settings. For some, nature is a landscape with no fences stretching far into the distance. Others will seek out a nature walk, where the path is clear and the area is managed. It could also come to mean a child discovering and revisiting a spider's web in the outdoor area.

Of course, the ways in which experiences are tied to children's learning and the support or guidance offered by educators is a central feature of nature-based practice, and this thread is regularly referred to here.

The term 'nature-based practice' is helpful in a number of ways:

✿ It recognises the value for young children playing and learning in nature.

✿ It concisely joins outdoor and indoor experiences.

✿ It centralises the role of nature within practical experiences.

✿ It allows for flexibility and is adaptable both across and within settings.

This chapter focuses on experiences aimed at or developed for children that seek to use nature as a resource to support learning.

The table on the following page shows the key components that we feel comprise nature-based practice and set it apart from other descriptions.

Manipulating sticks in the playground – in wild nature and indoors – joins this experience on multiple levels for children at Dunblane Nature Kindergarten.

Risk and challenge

There are tensions when considering risk and challenge in early years education, primarily that offering risk, which opens up the possibility of injury or harm. But the removal or reduction of exposure to risk can lead to environments that offer insufficient stimulation for children. Risky experiences, and reflection on what they have to offer and what they have taught each individual, are crucial in recognising how risk and challenge influence early years education and children's development.

Litigation and anxiety are pervasive features of contemporary society and attitudes towards children's risk-taking behaviours are a complex and hotly-debated topic. One perception of risk is visible when we look at how playgrounds or 'nature spaces' are available for learning and play; however, it is rare to see such spaces without a perimeter fence. These walls or boundaries serve a purpose for the adult — namely to dilute their risk-related angst.

Photo: Clare Nugent.

These children from a centre in Finland are trusted to be responsible for their own safety, including carrying their own spare clothing and the first-aid kit.

The key components of nature-based practice

Risk and challenge	Sustainability
Higher-level of risk-taking behaviours	Environmental awareness
Self-risk assessing and trust	Impact on land of early childhood provision
Collaborative (children supporting each other, cross-age working, educators engaging with colleagues)	Demonstrates ownership
	Linked learning: sow – harvest – forage – cook – eat – recycle/compost
Flexibility afforded by nature environments	**Culturally situated**
Encourages activity and exploration	The heritage of a place is included
Free from expectation and set learning goals	Adult as reproducer of social and cultural 'norms'
Freer from adult mediation	Tailoring practice to centralise local knowledge and culture
Offers time for reflection	Sensitive to the children in your setting and their experiences
Child- and nature-paced rather than curriculum-led	
Seeks child's voice	

Chapter 5 illustrates how an understanding of risk can be firmly embedded through experiences. This chapter focuses on children and their caregivers who have been tempted into wilder nature environments; hence we can discuss risk in terms of scaffolding children through a progression of challenging experiences. In this approach, progression is understood through children's prior experience and it tends to adopt a holistic view of children's development rather than consider specific outcomes.

A child with previous experience of playing in the sea will have knowledge about the waves and the power of the currents, while those new to the experience would need additional support to keep them as safe as necessary.

Little and Wyver (2008) reviewed studies and literature since 1990 and interpreted the findings in relation to early childhood education. They state that risky play is critical to children's healthy development, but that despite this, many early childhood educators and parents struggle to provide challenging and stimulating outdoor experiences for children. The reason for this, they propose, comes from restrictive regulations, risk-averse educators/adults and/or other social factors.

They emphasise the importance of considering risk within the larger context of children's development, as well as the need to focus on identifying and fostering a risk balance that is appropriate for each individual child.

Bringing together these points regarding risk, it is a concern that risk-averse or risk-avoidance strategies still often remain a central feature of early childhood. This presents multiple difficulties, including how adequate progression and layering of experiences can be shaped and provided for children. This is not a suggestion for a radical overhaul of practice. Rather, educators need to be sensitive to children's need for challenge and develop practice accordingly for each individual scenario.

Sustainability

Several texts on this topic are listed in the references. Of particular note for early childhood are Davis (2010) and Cutter-Mackenzie and colleagues (2013) who offer supporting guidance for those who seek to incorporate education for sustainability in their practice.

The Eco-schools programme is now well established in the UK as well as in European countries including Denmark, Germany and Greece. The programme makes links with the curriculum and offers a potential future route for early childhood educators as it involves different levels of schooling in many countries.

Chapter 2 explains that children who have first-hand experiences of nature also appreciate what it means to live sustainably. Such experience is vital when considering the contribution that nature-based learning can offer to sustainable lifestyles and the delivery of education for sustainability. Multiple forms of experiences feed into sustainability and include knowledge of the world around us, appreciation of the weather, knowledge of biodiversity and human impact on nature.

Flexibility afforded by nature environments

The outdoors comes in many forms and offers many flexible learning opportunities. Such flexibility is often labelled 'affordances', referring to work conducted in the 1970s that has since been interpreted in relation to education (Gibson, 1979).

Other material that influenced this perspective uses a variety of labels such as open-ended opportunities, unstructured play or play involving loose parts (Nicolson 1971). Broadhead (2003) coined the phrase 'anything-you-want-it-to-be-spaces' referring to indoor play and Tovey (2007) developed this to include playing outdoors.

Irrespective of what label or descriptions are used to explain children's play or interactions with nature, the common thread is that children can follow their interest and explore the properties of whatever is available to them in their outdoor space. For example, to an adult a stick is just that and often something to be removed from children's play, whereas to a child a stick can be used as a writing tool, a weapon, a magic wand, a stirrer or a tool to pick up bugs. Such resources can provide endless scope for play and learning. Of course experience plays a role in how play and learning may be shaped, and this is considered below.

Photo Clare Nugent.

Wherever children play in wild nature there will be an impact on the environment. In Finland, children jumping in the snow are aware of the new growth beneath, while in Australia children value the revegetation of sand dunes.

Photo: Clare Nugent

Access to loose natural material such as sticks, and even this rustic man-made log structure resembling a reindeer, are used in a variety of ways by the children without adult rules or restrictions, therefore increasing the play value of the opportunities.

Culturally situated

Children in countries where snow is a feature will traditionally make snow angels while children on beaches make sand angels. The action is the same but the natural material used is different. (Snow photo Clare Nugent.)

The role of culture is a vital component of outdoor experience and children's learning. This has been labelled 'culturally situated' to help include the influences of where practice occurs (place) and what has come before such experience.

Brown (2009), writing about outdoor adventure education, supports the idea that practices are culturally situated and historically constituted. It is inappropriate to merely note similarities, as practice cannot simply be copied or exported from one setting to another. To do so merely does a disservice to the people (adults and children) and processes involved in learning. Recently, Waite, Bølling & Bentsen (2015) recognise adopted provision 'reflect and refract the culture in which they are embedded' and we can explore this aspect of transfer through the example of Forest School.

In the UK, nature-based practice that accesses woodland spaces for early childhood education are most frequently reported through the concept of Forest School, that was brought to the UK from Denmark (Knight, 2011, 2013). Essentially, each Forest School is an interpretation of nature-based practice that originated in Denmark. This transfer means that whilst authors clarify the concept ethos and characteristics (Ridgers, Knowles & Sayers, 2012; Swarbrick, Eastwood & Tutton, 2004), examples in the UK are evolving somewhat differently from those in Denmark because of where they are located.

Working with young children on the Shetland Islands, folkloric traditions such as the Trow features in the children's play. This is a small, troll-like fairy creature, inclined to be short of stature, ugly and both shy and mischievous in nature.

Each of us as individuals go about our daily lives and interactions with others and in doing so, function within a layer of norms, beliefs and cultural expectations borne in part through our society's preferences and our personal experiences. These factors also have a bearing on early years education and thus, what works in one context may not have the same impact or offer the same kind of learning opportunities elsewhere.

Gulløv (2003) draws our attention to the significance of early childhood institutions as 'loci of cultural transmission' (p.26) where the heritage of history of places and people feeds into practice and is supported within children's experiences from an early age.

Despite the argument offered above that a situated view is needed when looking at early years education, there is value in comparison across practice as lessons can be drawn from sharing ideas. It is prudent to note that practice is not 'right' or 'wrong'. Rather, there are dimensions of resonance and difference to be shared and transferred among practitioners. In the words of a Danish practitioner:

> *We [in Denmark] have not found the golden stones, we may not be right, but it is just the way we do it. Here it is done differently, but we see the big, nature picture outside is the same.*
>
> MacQuarrie et al., 2015

Practitioners need to be sensitive and open to considering what nature-based practice can be in their own particular place, given their particular situation, including training, experience and local climate. We urge educators to see themselves as their own guide, combining expertise of their locality and their experience to date that has led them to their current forms of practice or ways of doing things.

Photo: Clare Nugent.

In many cultures and families there is already an outdoor culture, where children from a young age are included in outdoor experiences irrespective of the weather or time of day.

Photo: Clare Nugent.

It may be helpful for adults to get together in a supportive environment to share ideas and knowledge to reflect and expand on their own practice, while still being guided by their own beliefs and culture.

Just do it!

Children deserve the best; they deserve adults who will advocate for them, who will stand up for their rights to a high-quality childhood, who will move any barriers, even if 'creative' thinking is required! Children deserve this NOW. Trust your instinct, do your own research, use dynamic benefit-risk assessments. Above all, be brave, be courageous and then –

Just do it!

CASE STUDY 1

Setting:
Child First, Northampton, England

Practitioner interviewed:
Angela Green, manager

The children at Child First, Northampton have had access to natural indoor and outdoor areas since the setting was first opened by owner Tom Shea, in 2006.

The centre is set within three acres of wooded grounds with a range of different natural opportunities for the children to access on a daily basis.

Children of mixed age groups from zero to four years old access these areas daily and staff teams work together to observe and supervise play and exploration daily for as long as the children wish to remain there. We also offer Forest School sessions, normally run with groups of eight children aged three years and above, with a range of abilities including children with additional needs. These last for three hours and are run morning and afternoon.

The indoor spaces are homely and contain many examples of practical children's furniture and equipment thoughtfully designed by Tom and his team. Cots for babies are designed so that mobile babies can crawl into cosy spaces when tired, giving them a sense of agency.

A very apt invitation into the garden space with open spaces, mud kitchen, swings and a large selection of open-ended resources to encourage children to use their imagination.

Children have easy access to the large vegetable garden that is central to the natural practice.

A large wild wooded area with adventurous climbing and swinging opportunities available to children of all ages promotes imagination, gross motor development, balance and problem-solving skills through play.

Children, aged three years and over participating in the Forest School session also have time to freely explore the woodland and garden sites at other times.

Children may eat outdoors, and an outdoor sleeping hut was built, enabling children to sleep outdoors.

Opportunities for children

All areas of development are enhanced when using the outdoor environment. Children have the opportunity to risk take and be in charge of their own experiences. They learn to work together and also trust their own instincts.

CASE STUDY 2

Setting:
Riverside Cottage Nursery

Practitioner interviewed:
Luke Addison, manager

Riverside Cottage Nursery offers day care of children (fully private) including after-school and holiday club care. 15-20 children attend during the day, with an additional 10-15 after-schoolers arriving at 3.45pm.

Access to wild nature has been offered since opening in June 2011. There is a large focus on children having free-flow access to the available spaces all day:

> We access the spaces bordering our setting most days, if the children choose to. The dog needs to be walked every day anyway, so if nothing else, this gives children a daily opportunity to explore one of these spaces.

The length of time spent in the natural spaces changes, mainly dependent on the children's interests.

> We try to create time for children to become fully engrossed in their play and exploration, so we rarely set any 'times' for use of a particular space.

To further facilitate this, an outdoor toilet and the outdoor classroom was created so that:

> Even if children are cold or need shelter to do a particular activity (perhaps around something they have found, thought of or discovered in the woods) they don't have to disrupt their movement and thoughts by getting out of a puddle suit and wellies etc.

Luke settling where he has a good overview of the children's play in the stream, allowing them a perception of freedom from adult monitoring.

Meal times at Riverside Cottage are very flexible and designed to support children's engagement:

> We often have "rolling" snack where children can choose individually when best to have it, or indeed not at all. Lunch times, while we usually all sit together, are not strictly scheduled, so can be responsive to the overall needs of the setting that day.

There is also the option of taking a packed lunch, allowing groups to stay away the whole day.

The times spent at a particular site in wild nature vary from 15 minutes to the whole day; generally they prepare for at least four to five hours. The number of children going to one of the wild nature sites is flexible and varies; on average a group of about ten will set off together:

> This changes hugely depending on each occasion, time of year, weather, where we are going etc., but all children have the option to go. It would be unusual for less than four children to want to go and similarly unusual for everyone to want to go at the same time, but it does happen.

Riverside Cottage in its rural location has a wide range of outdoor spaces within the grounds as well as bordering the premises.

Within the grounds

> We have of course the 'normal' spaces found outside in early years settings, such as lawns and an area for wheeled toys. While this is useful and enjoyed by the children, we have many more spaces and experiences to offer that could be considered 'wild space' or that support our use of wild space.

The 'normal' outdoor space.

NBP VISION

Nature and the environment were very much a part of the initial vision of the setting. There was probably more emphasis on the individual learning and development side to start with e.g. tree climbing promotes gross motor skills, as we assumed this would be more attractive to parents. We also maintain ideas around how experiencing nature and wild spaces now builds a connection to the earth and much deeper, more intricate understandings of global citizenship – fairness, justice and equity. The idea is of course that along with other aspects of our practice, particularly pedagogies of power and critical thinking, this can encourage children to challenge the world around them, embrace radical change and contribute positively to the world.

Outdoor classroom

The outdoor classroom includes tools and a 'discovery area'. This is an interesting crossover space between inside and out.

It provides opportunities for children to take things from the outdoors and compare/contrast/measure/explore etc. This space also gives the children easy access to shelter and (slight) heat to warm up if needed. This means they do not have to get undressed from their waterproof suits and wellies, fragmenting the play/experience to go inside the building.

Sometimes children use it more as an inside space but with a stronger connection to nature and the outside world - hearing the extremes of the weather, feeling the wind move through and shake the structure, feeling the sun as it appears from behind clouds, hearing birds and foxes calling out and so much more.

Unstructured opportunities are offered in the outdoor classroom.

Large organic allotment

This is where they grow a lot of their own food and where the children are involved in the full seed-to-plate process. Luke discusses this in more detail in chapter 2.

Picking their own organic fruit such as apples and berries, children experience a true understanding of where food comes from.

Play that is self-directed and without adult intervention enables children to reach agreement with each other through mutual negotiation. This takes practice and more practice through play. These children have created a complex game around the boulders in the playground that involves many 'rules' they have made and then keep changing.

Upper Woodland

In the 'Upper Woodland' there is a wooded area with climbing equipment, rope swing, loose parts, mud kitchen, concrete blocks etc.

Many resources found here (with some possible exceptions) are increasingly found in lots of settings throughout Scotland.

Highly-physical play is regularly seen in the Upper Woodland along with construction, rules-based games, building obstacle courses, rope swings, team games, mud kitchen play and more.

A natural track leads from the Upper Woodland to the Lower Woodland site. Children of all ages may move out of sight from one space to the other with adults communicating via 'walkie talkie' to confirm safe arrival.

Lower Woodland

An additional acre of woodland, 'Lower Woodland' is much more focused on wild nature and natural experiences, including tree climbing, den making, fire building and exploration.

Children have access to risky opportunities in a supervised environment, enabling them to really test their courage and their limits. Climbing trees is fun, challenging and develops upper body strength and co-ordination.

Bordering the grounds

Beyond the fence (literally) children and practitioners have access to a river.

Over the fence in the woodland takes us to the Almond River and the public walks alongside it. The river, banks and walks are all used. Farm fields border the east of the grounds which provide huge open spaces - an inviting contrast to the woodland.

A calm and tranquil space for children to cool off on a hot day may change to a turbulent torrent after heavy rains. Benefit–risk assessments support and enable practitioners in their practice. Having access to the river supports children's sense of adventure, problem solving, balance and risk-assessing skills.

Across the road from the setting, we have the 161 hectare local nature reserve. This is a mixed site consisting of a previously worked peat bog, a remodelled oil shale bin and a sealed landfill site which has a cycle route and paths. This is a unique habitat with rare species which often encourages ideas and discussions around nature, biodiversity, carbon capture and storage and much more! There are also fantastic places to explore - we can see for miles to spot where in the county our house may be to the (very real) dangers of bogs and deep water.

We see ourselves on a continual journey as a setting and each adult working here, so many aspects of what we do are constantly evolving. We attempt to learn what we can from the great examples of practice all around the world and build on our practice through reflective processes and connection to our values/ethos.

One important aspect of our original vision that has grown is how we conceptualise childhood and the importance we place on the understanding of children as 'beings' as well as 'becomings'. It can be easy to forget that children's lives do not exist wholly as a preparation for adulthood - as a 'not quite' human. To this end, resources, experiences and activities are primarily in place because of children's interests, not because of whatever an adult thinks the child can gain from it developmentally.

Opportunities for children

The opportunities the setting offers children include:

- Den building
- Building fire (cooking food etc. included)
- Tree climbing
- Building (tree-houses, tarzan swings, concrete block work etc.)
- Water play in ponds, river, streams, bogs
- Mud play
- Exploration of nature and wild environments
- Multi-age play (from 2-12)
- Fishing
- Tool work
- Jobs/tasks (such as looking after the environment, litter picking, clearing the river, helping the farmer, highlighting issues to the community . . .)

More general opportunities include:

- Fun!
- Freedom, space and time to explore
- Discovery play
- Risk taking and management
- Unsupervised play
- Self-motivated challenge
- Social exploration - do/don't/should/shouldn't/right/wrong etc.
- Rule making
- Opportunity to do nothing in particular
- Guide their own learning
- Take part in project work - from having an idea to developing a project and arriving at a completed result
- Get hurt
- Fall out and experience conflict (and of course resolve it)
- Help others
- Be helped by others (including asking for it)
- Have ideas and test them out without judgement from others or loss of control to others
- Opportunities to fail (again and again) with an understanding that failing is hugely important.

CASE STUDY 3

Setting:
Home educator, Shetland Islands

Practitioner interviewed:
Alex Purbrick, mother and home educator

Each of the children have their own particular interests and passions, Alex would like them to find their own unique ways of connecting with nature.

Alex and her family live on the Shetland Islands where they are surrounded by large, natural, open spaces. She started taking each of her three children into wild spaces from birth. As soon as they could crawl they were encouraged to be on sand at the beach, on grass etc.

One precious memory is of our daughter, Dana, at eight months crawling out of the front door and up the gravel track towards the road to play with her brothers! Quite an achievement for that age! But the front door was always open so as babies they could learn their own boundaries (with my supervision obviously!) And decide for themselves to explore without me as an adult constantly telling them "No! You can't do this or go there!"

I will always be passionate about living the nature way, but I have realised, as my children grow older, that I would like them to discover their own unique ways of being in nature, of connecting with nature. For example my oldest son is passionate about fishing and being at sea on boats. These are two things I do not do, but I encourage him to do them because he is passionate about it. These are his unique ways in which he connects with nature and learns and has fun. So my role and vision as my children grow older is to gently direct them onto their own unique nature path of learning.

Alex and her three children, aged five, seven and nine try and go outside every day, irrespective of the weather, which can be extreme and challenging:

Some days in winter the rain is horizontal and the wind is hurricane force! So we see those days as perfect to cosy up inside and read or do crafts. In the winter we don't spend much time outdoors because there is not much shelter in the wild here from the wind and rain. In the summer we can be out for most of the day and sometimes take tents and camp. The sun in summer here can be very bright and intense because we are so far north.'

The children have access to large open spaces, where they can be free to run and BE in a way that comes naturally to them.

We have beautiful beaches in Shetland, so obviously we visit sand and stone beaches, exploring rock pools, animal life on the shore and, in the summer, swimming in the cold north Atlantic and being visited by seals!'

NBP VISION

To encourage my children to live the nature way! After writing the book 'The Nature Way' with my American friend, Corbin Harney, I realised how important it is to help children and adults live in a balanced way with nature. I feel nature is our greatest teacher and I wanted my children to experience this, to understand how nature can comfort our emotions as well as ignite our passions and desire for learning as we travel on our life path.

We visit tree plantations for our forest experiences although they are not really forests, but small woods! We go walking through heather moorlands, through the hills, exploring prehistoric rock formations and ancient ruins. We also spend the summer up our peat hill where we cut peat to burn as fuel, so the kids play with the peat, paddle in the shallow watery bogs, have picnics there and pitch tents. Also there is a small quarry near our house where the kids go to play. We study the tadpoles living there in spring. The puddles of water are frozen in winter so they skate on them and play on the ice.

Opportunities for children

To discover and learn from nature. To play and create with their imagination. To be immersed in the wildness of nature, meeting wild animals, for example seals, birds, otters, as well as shellfish, insects and the plant world. We forage for wild food in spring, summer, autumn (not so much in winter!). So the kids learn what plants grow at certain times of the year and how we can harvest them and how to cook them. They also forage for shellfish on the shoreline, for example whelks, razorclams, mussels. They learn how nature can support them through food, and especially the importance of the ocean due to us living on an island surrounded by water. The sea is a great teacher for them.

Having the freedom of wild nature children can be boisterous, participate in large movements involving the whole body, and they can also be quiet and reflective. Nature caters for everybody.

CASE STUDY 4

Setting:
Dream Days, Northumberland, England

Practitioner interviewed:
Kimberley Wilford, Creator

Kimberley cares for six children aged from nine months to school age within her home. Prior to starting her own service she worked at Child First, Northumberland for eight years where:

> They take outdoor play very seriously and understand the importance.

At Dream Days the children have access to the garden and wild spaces throughout the day. The programme is led by the children, so they have the choice and will stay outdoors until they themselves decide to go indoors.

Children have a natural fascination with fire and water; supporting these fascinations in a supervised environment allows them to safely explore these exciting elements.

> I have had children the last couple of days helping to turn the garden into the space they want it to be. During this process the children have helped burn the old wood, move the bricks, climb trees and found lots of bugs. Risky play in the outdoor space is going to be a main priority.
>
> Within walking distance we have the embankment where the children and I walk to feed the swans and ducks, a local park where we explore the wildlife, and our garden where we have fruit trees, and have just made a growing patch and various digging spaces for the children to explore further.

Children have access to sticks and use these for a variety of purposes. This little girl is delighted with having balanced a stick between two posts, a great problem-solving opportunity.

Real life experiences, including having direct contact with farm animals, form part of Kimberley's programme.

NBP VISION

My vision is to create a space where the children develop by exploring natural resources and environments, enabling them to learn about the world while boosting their brain development even further. This vision has come from the Child First philosophy, where I was moulded as a practitioner. I am not one to allow my children to sit indoors watching television, playing on computer games because research shows that the natural environment is crucial for holistic development. A space where they can use all their senses while learning life skills.

Opportunities for children

The children:

> Climb trees, grow food, dig for bugs, cook on fire, use natural, open ended materials for large-scale construction and participate in risky play opportunities.

Even the youngest children are able to explore in a hands-on, sensorial manner while dressed appropriately for the weather and the opportunity.

Children are trusted to lead the way through the autumn leaves, giving them a sense of freedom and ownership in this sensorial natural space.

This baby is included in the motivational experience while feeding the swans with the older children.

Photographs supplied by Kimberley Wilford

CASE STUDY 5

Setting:

Dunblane Nature Kindergarten, Scotland

Practitioner interviewed:

Steven White, project co-ordinator

Steven has been working with children in a nature kindergarten setting since 2000. In 2013 he introduced the concept to a local nursery which, through his passion and commitment and the support of the owners and other educators, became Dunblane Nature Kindergarten. The centre offers wrap around, full day care for 95 children aged from six months to five years from 7.30am until 6.30pm.

Dunblane Nature Kindergarten is centrally situated in the town of Dunblane, and a high value is based on their links to the local community where the children are often seen and welcomed as they walk to the stream, primary school, post office or shops.

As well as having a strong nature-based approach, the setting also has a strong philosophy in maintaining respectful relationships between adults and children, amongst adults themselves and in supporting children to develop the same respectful relationships between themselves. This philosophy is central to holistic sustainability and therefore links strongly to the nature-based philosophy and approach.

There is always time for a comforting cuddle with Steven and his responsive team. Working in the time that is best suited to young children means slowing down the pace and working in nature time.

NBP VISION

To provide children and adults with an engaging and meaningful experience through an outdoor educational approach.

The journey for Dunblane Nature Kindergarten started in 2013 when Steven and his team 're-natured' the existing non-natural playground to support the new nature-based philosophy of the setting.

In the forest a group of two-year-old children learn about small fires and cooking their own marshmallows to make S'mores.

Indoor spaces include kitchens open to the children. The centre's respectful theme is reflected in the detail, such as table cloths and flowers on the tables.

On the website the philosophy is clearly explained:

> We encourage children to grow through their exploration and discovery of knowledge through enlightenment and curiosity. Highly trained staff will nurture and support your child, through subtle guidance of a philosophical approach through open-ended questioning. Creating a respectful dialogue with your child, our staff will ignite their human inquiry. Developing and promoting challenging experiences for your child, through higher order thinking resources, challenging outdoor spaces and calming indoor classrooms.

The challenging outdoor spaces include the naturalistic garden space with many exciting and risky opportunities, as well as the range of wild nature spaces the children spend considerable time in every day.

The fire is a central feature of the playground with children of all ages 'helping' or just 'hanging out' next to the fire. Food such as baked potatoes is cooked for lunch, and children and adults will share lunch together, often outside. Children are respected and trusted to use 'real' plates and glasses.

The garden space includes a large sandpit, informal garden beds, water children can access and natural loose parts.

The garden space is compact and now offers a very natural environment. The concrete and wet pour surfaces, as well as the static playground equipment, have been removed and replaced with grass, soil and natural functional structures. With the heavy wear and tear visible and the 'kid erosion' in certain spaces it is obvious that the children spend most of their time outdoors in all weathers, it would be fair to say that the grass struggles to grow in some spaces! The children aged from six months are highly engaged; all, including the babies, are appropriately dressed for the environment and the weather.

Providing high-quality, appropriate outdoor clothing is considered a priority enabling all children and adults to be comfortable outdoors.

The outdoor classroom is functional; children have ownership, and it features in many of the imaginative games the children play. Wheelbarrows filled with logs became presents which were arranged on the floor to create enclosures, with natural materials, such as leaves, purposefully arranged within.

The children access green spaces such as parks, river walks and open gardens in and around the town of Dunblane. They also spend daily, prolonged periods of time in nearby wilderness spaces with streams, rivers, hills, scrub and wildlife, staying in these spaces for as long as they wish. Children access these wild spaces in their own time; it is about the journey and not so much about reaching an end point. At times a walk to the stream may only be 50 meters before children discover something that interests them and then spend the next few hours in that spot.

What is significant about the Dunblane Nature Kindergarten journey is that one practitioner with a strong vision on nature-based practice and who advocated for this change to benefit the children, was able to work with the existing team of educators and managers and, together, they were able to make a difference, to convert this centre into an award-winning nature-based setting. Juliet Robertson commented:

> The staff at this nursery demonstrate that significant lasting changes are possible to make that do not involve hiring a new set of staff, but rather, giving everyone the respect, responsibility and trust to make these changes. The sense of empowerment is strong. "Everyone has a sense of entitlement. It's a big family. I can't see any of us moving to another nursery."

Opportunities for children

> To be themselves and follow their own inquiry in a nurturing environment.

At Dunblane Nature Kindergarten practitioners are responsive to individual children's needs and interests, reading a story to a small group in a space they choose, rather than a formal whole group.

A pathway adjacent to the centre leads to a variety of wild spaces, including the river. Children appreciate the large open spaces; and the same respectful trust shown towards them within the setting is also shared in these spaces.

Setting:

The Orchard Nature Nursery, Dumfries, Scotland

Practitioner interviewed:

Kim Bannister, owner/manager

The Orchard Nature Nursery offers full day care to 35 children aged from zero to five years and started taking children out into wild nature in 2013.

The children have daily access to varying wild spaces every day, ranging from the garden/estate grounds to the forest or beach where they stay all day if that is their choice. Child's comment:

We eat our lunch in the garden.

Our garden offers a large natural play space, no pre-made play structures, we offer loose parts (tyres, bread crates, guttering, wood off cuts).

Exploring malleable material such as mud and clay is an extension to investigating mixtures in a mud kitchen, offered in this nature-based setting.

NBP VISION

For children to access free-flow outdoor experiences throughout the day, using our child-led, child-initiated approach.

Accessing the natural outdoor environment in all weathers offers children the opportunity to discover and compare changes brought on by the weather.

Children have regular access to the local beach, which offers a whole new dimension to their already-rich natural experiences. Scrambling across the rough rocks requires children to be good self-risk assessors. Child's comment: 'We know how to keep safe.'

Having the opportunity to bring knowledge gained in other spaces adds another dimension to the children's learning and experiences.

Opportunities for children

In the garden:

> Mud kitchen, wood work, sand, water play (using rain water if possible) construction (loose parts) physical (bikes/balance beams) art, fire building and cooking.

The children visit a local forest which is only a ten-minute walk away, a small woodland area where children can explore the diverse nature and changes available.

> We are located on a private estate so we can access the grounds and gardens at any point – this gives us access to large green space, rock garden area and a waterfall.

On the estate:

> Physical play (ball games/hide and seek/parachute) nature hunts, walks, visit the local park, paddling in the waterfall, investigate water movement (stream)

> Forest – den building, literacy (story telling/story stones) art, numeracy (measuring).

Kim is beach-school trained which gives her the confidence to:

On the beach:

> Also access a local beach which is a 20-minute drive away, this offers rock pools, caves etc.

> Rock pooling, water movement, safety, shell identification, caves, sand/rock art, mark making.

Being part of the magnificence of the ocean while having trusted adults sensitive to individuals nearby offers safety as well as a sense of adventure.

Providing opportunities for children to explore flowers and other vegetation closely in their play creates a deep sensory and scientific knowledge of the plants. Child's comment: 'I'm making a secret potion'.

Babies and toddlers are able to explore their natural environment in an age-appropriate and sensorial manner.

Photographs provided by Kim Bannister

Setting:
Nature Nurture, Aberdeen, Scotland

Practitioner interviewed:
Terri Harrison, project co-ordinator, early intervention

> The Nature Nurture® Project provides an early intervention programme for children and young people, comprising the restorative effects of free play in a natural environment and closely attuned nurturing interactions with specially trained staff. The project facilitates the development of resilience in the most vulnerable, such as children and young people from families affected by substance misuse, alcohol abuse, domestic violence, abusive relationships, neglect and poverty. The project has worked successfully with children from Aberdeen's most deprived areas and has worked closely with the children's families, social workers and school staff.
>
> (Website)

On the journey to the woodland children are made aware of possible hazards and are supported to try and keep themselves safe. These young children are shown trust, allowing them to make the decision if it is safe to cross the road within the setting.

Terri started taking children out into the wild spaces in 2006. Nature Nurture offers vulnerable children access to the nature spaces once a week. The children aged two to five years old, five to eight years old and eight to eleven years old stay for half a day during the term time, while during the school holidays whole day sessions are run. Each session is attended by ten children.

The property consists mainly of woodland areas, but Nature Nurture involves a journey through mixed environments including farmland, field, riverside, meadow and parkland.

Children will often take ownership of the trolley – until they choose not to. Adults recognise this choice and may then help until another child or group offers to help. Moving the resources is a collaborative effort.

Terri supporting a young child who has requested support. Children are encouraged to be independent while at the same time always having a responsive adult near them. At times children need not so much the physical help but need to know that the adult is beside them for emotional comfort.

NBP VISION

To provide opportunities for children from challenging circumstances to have free play and nurturing in natural environments. Our sessions are designed to support and promote each child's resilience and wellbeing. Our vision has remained the same but our understanding of resilience and how this can be supported by time spent in nature has deepened over the years.

Children are met off the bus by welcoming adults, aware of every individual child's needs and preferences. All-weather clothing is prepared in advance considering the individual child; adults calmly support each child as they prepare to go out.

Opportunities for children

Opportunities for free play and child-initiated learning. Sessions allow for social interaction and practising social skills. Children have the opportunity to learn new skills and develop talents and interests such as arts, craft, animal care, and develop physical skills such as climbing trees, building shelters and lighting and using fire for cooking and craft. Children also have the opportunity to develop a connection to and understanding of the natural world.

The highly-skilled adults working with the children are calm and focussed; voices are not raised and there does not appear to be a sense of urgency. At the end of the session Terri calls the group together with a familiar sound to them, indicating that it is time to gather.

High adult to child ratios in this programme for the older children allows them increased freedom while at the same time the possibility of increased structure and support, depending on individual needs.

Nature Nurture offers a range of free play as well as adults modelling an intentional skill while children connect to nature.

Setting:
Alfreton Nursery School, Alfreton, England

Practitioner interviewed:
Angela Stanton, headteacher

Grass left to grow, sticks left on the ground and a newly-added pond all add to the wild feel of this space, which will continue to increase as it evolves over time.

Alfreton Nursery School is a Derbyshire local authority nursery school where children have been able to access wild nature since 2003.

Every week two sessions are run: one in the morning and one in the afternoon for different groups of children. Each Forest School session lasts for two and a half hours and is attended by 12 children aged three and four years old. Every child in the nursery is given the opportunity to attend at least 20 sessions during their time in nursery.

We also use this area for targeted children in small groups: the Earth Elves! Another 4 sessions during the week.

Future plans include continuing to develop the site to include a new fernery, hedgehog habitat, pond exploration, further expansion of the mud pie kitchen (using recycled materials) with the help of local builders, and a new creek for water play.

As a new Teaching School we will be able to share our Forest School and learning experience with other schools, helping to encourage more establishments to provide Forest School and outdoor learning experiences for their children.

We initially took children and their families, including grandparents, to a local woodland, using a minibus to access the site. This was cleared and managed by environmental services and had public access via a nearby pathway. We gradually developed this site to include a big log circle and a permanent shelter with the children. We remained on this site for eight years before deciding to extend and develop Forest Schools, and the environments needed to support this, within our own school grounds.

'We already had a developing Forest School site that began with obtaining a piece of field from the local secondary school and set about changing it to become an early woodland area. Our Forest School site was emerging.'

'We supported local groups to engage and develop our site, including the Probation Service; giving positive skills to young offenders as they fenced, built, planted trees and helped to create our fantastic bug wall structure.'

Fruit trees where children are able to experience the cycle of growing fruit; harvesting, eating and composting.

Natural pathways amongst the mature trees and a structure to encourage bugs into the space.

NBP VISION

Our initial vision was to take children once a week on a minibus to a local woodland area to experience a Forest School learning outdoors experience. This was in addition to a well-resourced, on-site outdoor area. We now have a constantly changing, well established on-site Forest School and an outdoor ethos which is fully embedded throughout school. The time saved on travelling to our original Forest School site allows children to spend more time in our on-site Forest School.

We used a local garden centre to gradually add more trees to the woodland and a local business continually supports and helps with sourcing of new, exciting natural materials for our Forest School. Local business partners and builders are now contributing to the site's continuous development and support us with its maintenance. As part of their community cohesion work, local businesses have also offered two community days where a whole workforce has been provided to develop new projects and initiatives. All these local links have gradually evolved over a long time to become part of a bigger community team that supports our Nursery School and the developments within it.

Our Forest School area includes a mud pie kitchen, log circle (with fire building equipment), a permanent shelter and feeding stations that the children love to explore and play amongst.

The large natural playground offers children daily free access to natural elements including logs, willow shelters and a large sand-play space.

Regular forest school sessions are offered by the experienced team, three of whom have completed Forest School training.

The woodland space inspired us to obtain another much larger field, again from the neighbouring secondary school, which has been gradually developed over the last four years. This provides trees, a recycled greenhouse, allotment, new habitat spaces and willow structures.

The school also has a natural outdoor play area, as well as a space

Which is an orchard with willow tunnel, log circle and mud kitchen which is available for free play.

Opportunities for children

Angela Stanton identified the contribution to children's emotional well-being through:

- Pond exploration
- Tree climbing
- Imaginative play
- Immersion in wildlife, to foster respect of creatures and their habitats.
- Sensory learning opportunities throughout all seasons
- Fire building, cooking on the fire and fire safety
- Using tools safely
- Den building
- Treasure hunts
- Confidence building through new challenges/learning new skills
- Having a joyful experience, without pressure
- Breathing in fresh air and resistance to colds.

CASE STUDY 9

Setting:
Abacus Filton Hill Preschool, Bristol, England

Practitioner interviewed:
Annette Parsons, manager

Abacus Filton Hill is situated with the primary school and open during the school terms. They cater for 20 children every day aged from two to five years old. The children access wild nature every day for at least two and a half hours.

Annette herself has always loved the outdoors – she and her children love to walk! The wild spaces they have access to are many and varied including:

> Woods, brooks, steep banks and hills, streams, rivers, fields and wild open spaces.

The children have access to natural and man-made loose parts, encouraging free exploratory play for all ages. Combine these loose parts with water and opportunities are endless.

NBP VISION

Freedom to explore! More time to explore!

Water in its many forms is always a great attraction to young children. As one of the natural elements, its fluidity and ability to take on the 'shape' of the environment brings out the scientific investigator in children as they engage in joyful play.

Opportunities for children

- Freedom from adults telling them what they can and cannot do.

- Thinking for themselves.

- Sensory connection with nature.

- An opportunity to shut down from the outside world.

Setting:
Boldon Nursery School: Outdoor Nursery, South Tyneside, England

Practitioner interviewed:
Sue Stokoe, headteacher

The children have had access to wild natural spaces in this school since 2010. There are 48 children aged three to four years old in each session. They have continuous access to the garden and wild spaces within the setting, children who attend full days (40%) could choose to be outdoors for six hours a day while others who attend for three hours daily could spend all that time outdoors.

The children have access to a range of different natural spaces; onsite, in the local environment and further away.

A big part of the culture here in South Tyneside is the sea and the sand. Most children live only a short bus ride away from their local beach. We visit these beaches with our children. Our local beach has a very famous lighthouse, Souter lighthouse of which we have a replica in our own beach back at nursery. When children visit the beach they have access to sand, dunes, the sea, rock pools, the lighthouse.

Most communities within South Tyneside have a local burn/park within them. We have one near to our nursery which is within walking distance. The burn has a stream through it, trees (various types) to climb, a copse, hills and flat landscapes. Water voles, wild flowers and plants, weeds and nettles are in abundance.

We also have our very own wild space on site, filled with trees to climb, birds, hedgehogs, frogs, tadpoles, shrubs, flowers /wild plants, a fire pit, beach, mud and puddles in abundance.'

How often do children have access to these wild spaces?

- *We access our own wild space, all day, every day, whatever the weather.*

- *We may visit the other sites with a small learning group or the whole class. Visits offsite to the coast incur travel costs, which limits the amount of times we can go out. (The nursery is in an area of deprivation and parents cannot help towards these costs.)*

- *We can walk to the local burn and go there more regularly, for some children, weekly. The burn is an area children would go to with their parents in the evening or weekends.*

NBP VISION

To create a place where children have time and space to explore their interests and fascinations, where childhood is celebrated. To use nature, its seasons and elements as a provocation for the learning for children, parents and staff. [This] continues to embed and inspire our practice.

Children and chickens, a winning combination. Caring for birds and animals in a hands-on and authentic manner promotes empathy, caring and responsibility, important values cultured in a natural environment.

Opportunities for children

The opportunities the setting offers are:

- playing
- climbing
- paddling
- exploring
- whittling

- representing /creating
- cooking
- eating
- talking

- negotiating
- cooperating
- using real tools
- research

Personal connections, relationships and close bonds are formed in the outdoors through facing experiences and challenges together in Boldon Nursery School's natural garden.

Photos provided by Sue Stokoe

The joy of running through the willow tunnel on a carpet of autumn leaves can clearly be seen in this capture at Boldon School Nursery.

A wooden cabin with a warm cosy space for children to shelter and snuggle up in and warm up on a cold day.

Creating a wild space within the outdoor space allows children to have continuous access to exciting natural and hidden spaces.

Negotiating a wet, slippery log is excitingly challenging; every child approaches this in a way that is developmentally appropriate for that individual child

A wooden structure offers shelter around the fire pit.

Risk assessment

Such benefit-risk assessments are often viewed as too onerous, in reality, once documented, these only need to be reviewed which does not mean redoing the whole document but, as a team, deciding what changes should be made and dating the new document.

Activity Benefit Risk Assessment

Activity/opportunity: Tree climbing

With this benefit risk assessment document, we evidence the thinking and planning that has gone into considering this opportunity for children. We have used our professional judgement to weigh up the benefits and the risks and have put control measures in place to reduce the risks to an acceptable level without substantially removing the benefits of the opportunity to children. As children's behaviour and changes in the environment may be unpredictable we recognise that adults will continue to dynamically risk assess the opportunity on the day. This document is reviewed annually or sooner if an incident or change occurs. The information is communicated to families and children. It is sighted and signed by adults working with the children.

Educator/s: N. Buchan, S Robertson		
Date of assessment: 15.01.16	Due date of revision: 14.01.17	Any other documents attached? Excursion BRA if appropriate

Benefits of the activity: We have considered this opportunity and have identified the following benefits to the children

Fun, promotes emotional and physical well being, development of gross and fine motor co-ordination, exercise and movement, allows children to challenge themselves and to develop self-risk assessing skills, children develop an awareness of some of the hazards related to tree climbing, children develop and improve physical motor skills, children develop self confidence and self esteem which leads to increased emotional and physical wellbeing, develop group awareness and co-operation, children will develop an awareness of seasonal changes and the changes brought on by different weather, develop awareness of the characteristics of trees such as branches, bark, textures, seeds, fruit.

Children's comments: We see children as capable and competent, able to assess benefits as well as the hazards and risks appropriately for their age

Harry 2: "I climb up"   Oskar 3: " To the top, to the top...but don't jump"   Phillip 3: "My cat climbs high, to the top"
Dillon 4: " trees give you air to breathe, if we didn't have trees we can't breathe"
Melanie 4: "I can't climb with a dress, only shorts"   Sarah: "only climb as high as you feel safe"

©nikibuchannaturallearning2016

Hazards Identified:	Precautions/Control measures:	Who/when:	Risk before contr. meas	Risk after contr. meas
Debris on the bush/garden floor	Raise awareness of trip hazard. Remove where appropriate and children can't access severity of risk	Educator & Children – on arrival and ongoing	High	Low
Dead wood in tree canopy and dead branches in climbing area	Remove dead wood if appropriate and /or avoid the hazard area. Raise awareness of possible fragility of dead wood with children.		Extreme	High
Slippery surfaces	Raise children's awareness of the hazard and allow self-evaluation. Support children in evaluating weather conditions.		Extreme	High
Drop heights	Support children to self-risk assess and judge own ability. Monitor landing location and involve children in removing serious hazards or change landing location. Support children where requested.		Extreme	High
Protruding branches/sticks	Remove serious hazards children will not be aware of through consultation with children allowing them to evaluate and self-risk assess		Moderate	Low
Unstable/diseased tree	Contact tree expert to assess tree if to be accessed regularly. If identified during an excursions, avoid area and raise awareness of additional hazard with children	Niki contact "stickman" 16.01.16	Extreme	High

Risk Matrix:

Likelihood					
Rare	Unlikely	Possible	Likely	Almost certain	
Low	Low	Low	Moderate	Moderate	Insignificant
Low	Low	Moderate	Moderate	High	Minor
Low	Moderate	High	High	High	Moderate
Moderate	High	High	Extreme	Extreme	Major
High	High	Extreme	Extreme	Extreme	Catastrophic

(Consequences / Risk Matrix)

First Aid kit is found: In the office and in excursion backpack
Emergency contact details are found: In the office and in excursion backpack
Adults with First Aid training: Niki, Sue, Mark, Sam
Emergency contact number: 000
Hospital emergency number: 03 28654

Notes: Peter has epilepsy currently controlled – monitor closely when climbing trees
Signed:

©nikibuchannaturallearning2016

A PRACTICAL GUIDE TO Nature-Based Practice

References and further reading

A.A. Milne, Winnie-the-Pooh, 1926

Aaron Harmer, Australian spiders: the 10 most dangerous by Clémentine Thuilier, August 16, 2012, Australian Geographic, http://www.australiangeographic.com.au/topics/wildlife/2012/08/australian-spiders-the-10-most-dangerous/

Ball, D., Gill, T., Spiegal, B. 2008, *Managing Risk in Play Provision: Implementation guide*. Play England, Crown/Play England/Big Lottery Fund copyright

Beames, S., Higgins, P. J. & Nicol, R. 2011, *Learning Outside the Classroom: Theory and Guidelines for Practice*. Taylor & Francis

Bird, W. 2007, Natural England and the Royal Society for the Protection of Birds (RSPB)

Blake, S., Welch, D. M. 2006, *Making Fire. An Essential Survival Guide*. Published by David M. Welch 2006 Australian Aboriginal Culture Series No 2

Bodrova, E. & Leong, D. J. 2005, Uniquely preschool: What research tells us about the ways young children learn. *Educational Leadership*, 63(1), 44–47

Borradaile, L. 2006, *Forest School Scotland: An Evaluation*. Foresty Commission Scotland

Broadhead, P. 2003, *Early Years Play and Learning: Developing Social Skills and Cooperation*. Taylor & Francis

Brown, M. 2009, Reconceptualising outdoor adventure education: Activity in search of an appropriate theory. *Australian Journal of Outdoor Education*, 13(2), 3–13

Buchan, N. 2015, *Children in Wild Nature, A practical guide to nature-based practice in Australia and New Zealand*. Teaching Solutions

Burroughs, John, 1919, Field and Study, Cambridge, MA: Riverside Press.

Care Inspectorate, My World Outdoors, sharing good practice in how early years services can provide play and learning wholly or partially outdoors. Published by Communications

Carr 1997, p. 10, cited in Stephenson, 2003, p. 41

Carr, M. Lee, W., 2001, Learning Stories, Constructing Learner Identities in Early Education, Sage

Claxton, G. & Carr, M. 2004, A framework for teaching learning: learning dispositions. *Early Years International Journal of Research and Development*, 24(1) 87–97

Copeland, K. A., Sherman, SN., Kendeigh, BA. Kalkwarf, HJ. Saelens, BE. Societal Values and Policies May Curtail Preschool Children's Physical Activity in Child Care Centers

Csikszentmihayli, M. 1979, The Concept of Flow, in B. Suttin Smith (Ed) *Play and Learning*, London, Gardner Press.

Cutter-Mackenzie, A. & Edwards, S. 2013, Toward a model for early childhood environmental education: Foregrounding, developing, and connecting knowledge through play-based learning. *The Journal of Environmental Education*, 44(3), 195–213

Davis, J. M. 2010, *Young Children and the Environment: Early Education for Sustainability*. Cambridge University Press.

Davis, J. M. & Elliott, S. 2004, Mud pies and daisy chains: Connecting young children and nature. *Every Child*, 10(4), 4-5.

Deviney, J., Duncan, S., Harris, S., Rody, M. & Rosenberry, L. 2010, *Inspiring Spaces for Young Children*. Silver Spring USA: Gryphon House

Einarsdóttir, J. & Wagner, J. T. 2006, *Nordic Childhoods and Early Education: Philosophy, Research, Policy, and Practice in Denmark, Finland, Iceland, Norway, and Sweden*. IAP-Information Age Pub

Fägerstam, E. 2012a, Children and young people's experience of the natural world: Teachers' perceptions and observations. *Australian Journal of Environmental Education*, 28(01), 1–16

Fägerstam, E. 2012b, Space and Place: Perspectives on outdoor teaching and learning. Master in Outdoor Environmental Education and Outdoor Life, Lindköping University

Fjørtoft, I. 2001, The Natural Environment as a Playground for Children: The Impact of Outdoor Play Activities in Pre-Primary School Children. *Early Childhood Education Journal*, 29(2), 111–117

Fjørtoft, I. & Sageie, J. 2000, The natural environment as a playground for children: Landscape description and analyses of a natural playscape. *Landscape and Urban Planning*, 48(1), 83–97

Fleer, M., Hedegaard, M. & Tudge, J. 2012, World Yearbook of Education 2009: *Childhood Studies and the Impact of Globalization: Policies and Practices at Global and Local Levels*. Taylor & Francis

Gardner, H 1999, Intelligence Reframed: *Multiple Intelligences for the 21st Century*. New York: Basic Books

Gibson, J. J. 1979, *The Ecological Approach to Visual Perception*. Hillsdale NJ: Lawrence Erlbaum

Gill, T. 2007, *No Fear: Growing up in a Risk Averse Society*, London: Calouste Gulbenkian Foundation

Gill. T. 2012, Blog 'Rethinking Childhood' 25 July

Gopinath, B., Baur, L. A., Wang, J. J., Hardy, L. L., Teber, E., Kifley, A., et al. 2011, Influence of Physical Activity and Screen Time on the Retinal Microvasculature in Young Children. *Arteriosclerosis, Thrombosis, and Vascular Biology*, 31(5), 1233

Grahn, P., Martensson, F., Llindblad, B., Nilsson, P., & Ekman, A. 1997, The natural environment as a playground for children: The impact of outdoor play activities in pre-primary school children. *Early Childhood Education Journal*, 29(2): 111–17. UTE pa DAGIS, Stad & Land nr. 93/1991 Sveriges lantbruksuniversitet, Alnarp

Gray, P. 2014, Risky Play: Why Children Love It and Need It. Blog post published 7 April in Freedom to Learn 5

Gulløv, E. 2003, Creating a natural place for children: an ethnographic study of Danish Kindergartens, in Fog Olwig, K. & Gulløv, E. (eds) *Children's Places. Cross-cultural Perspectives.* London: Routledge

Harney, C., Purbrick, A. 2009, *The Nature Way.* University of Nevada Press

Hedegaard, M. & Fleer, M. 2008, Family practices and how children are positioned as active agents, in M. Fleer, M. Hedegaard, & J. Tudge, (eds) *World Yearbook of Education 2009: Childhood Studies and the Impact of Globalization: Policies and Practices at Global and Local Levels.* Taylor & Francis

Henwood, K. L. & Pidgeon, N. F. 1998, The place of forestry in modern Welsh culture and life. Report to the Forestry Commission. Bangor: University of Wales, School of Psychology

Hughes, B. & Melville, S. 1996, *Play Environments: A Question of Quality*, PLAYLINK, London

Hunt, A., Stewart, D., Burt, J. & Dillon, J. (2016). 'Monitor of Engagement with the Natural Environment: a pilot to develop an indicator of visits to the natural environment by children - Results from years 1 and 2' (March 2013 to February 2015). Natural England Commissioned Reports, Number 208

Ingold, T. 2000, *Perception of the Environment: Essays in Livelihood, Dwelling and Skill.* London: Routledge

Jackson, N., Play Development Manager, Learning Trust. Climbing trees – risk and adventure. http://loveoutdoorplay.net/2012/03/26/climbingtree

Kaarby, K. M. E. 2005, Children playing in nature. Questions of Quality, 121

Kahn Jr, P. H. & Kellert, S. R. 2002, *Children and Nature: Psychological, Sociocultural, and Evolutionary Investigations.* MIT Press

Kaplan, R. & Kaplan, S. 1989, *The Experience of Nature: A Psychological Perspective.* Cambridge University Press

Kellert, S. R. 2012, The Naturalistic Necessity, in Dunlap, J. & Kellert, S. R. (eds) *Companions in Wonder: Children and Adults Exploring Nature Together.* MIT Press

Kellert, S. R. 2002, Experiencing Nature: Affective, Cognitive, and Evaluative Development, Children and Nature: *Psychological, Sociocultural, and Evaluative Investigations*, Cambridge, MA: The MIT Press.

Knight, S. 2011, Forest Schools for All. Sage Publications

Knight, S. 2013, *Forest School and Outdoor Learning in the early Years.* SAGE Publications Ltd

Kuo ,F. E & Faber A. 2004, *A potential natural treatment for attention deficit/hyperactivity disorder: Evidence from a national study*, American Journal of public Health, 94,9

Lady Allen of Hurtwood. Junkyard Playgrounds. Time. 25 June 1965. www.time.com/time/magazine/article/0,9171,833789,00.html, 22 April 2011

Laevers, F.1994. the Innovative Project Experiential Education and the Definition of Quality in Education, in Laevers, F. (Ed) Defining and Assessing quality in early Childhood Education. Studia paedagogica. Leuven, Leuven University Press.

Lester, S. & Maudsley, M. 2007, Play Naturally. *A Review of Children's Natural Play.* Play England

Lester, S. & Russell, S. 2008, Play for a change. Play policy and practice: A review of contemporary perspectives. Play England. Retrieved 21.6.2010 from www.worldleisure.org/pdfs/Copy%20of%20book_rev_play_for_change.pdf

Little, H. & Wyver, S. 2008, Outdoor Play: Does Avoiding the Risks Reduce the Benefits? *Australian Journal of Early Childhood*, 33(2), 33–40

Louv, R. 2005, *Last Child in the Woods: Saving Our Children from Nature-deficit Disorder.* Chapel Hill NC: Algonquin Books of Chapel Hill

Macnaghten, P. & Urry, J. 1998, *Contested Natures*: SAGE Publications

MacQuarrie, S., Nugent, C., & Warden, C. (2015). Learning with nature and learning from others: nature as setting and resource for early childhood education. *Journal of Adventure Education & Outdoor Learning*, 15(1), 1–23

Malaguzzi, L. 1998, 'History, ideas and philosophy', in Edwards, C. Gandini, L. & Forman, G. 1998, *The Hundred Languages of Children: The Reggio Emilia Approach.* Ablex Publishing, Greenwich p.83

Marjanovic, L. & Fekonja, U. 2007, Characteristtics of children's language during free play and other preschool activities, in Jambor, T. & van Gils, J. (eds) *Several Perspectives on Children's Play: Scientific Reflections for Practitioners.* Antwerp: Coronet Books Incorporated

Maudsley, MJ (ed) 2005, Playing on the Wildside: An essential resource for environmental playwork. Cheltenham: Playwork Partnerships. http://www.playworkpartnerships .co.uk/

Maynard, T. 2007, Making the best of what you've got': adopting and adapting the Forest School approach, in Austin, R. (ed.) *Letting the Outside in: Developing Teaching And Learning Beyond the Early Years Classroom.* Stoke on Trent: Trentham Books Limited

Nicholson, S., 1971, *How Not To Cheat Children: The Theory of Loose Parts*, Landscape Architecture. 62 30-5

Nilsen, R. D. 2008, Children in nature: Cultural ideas and social practices in Norway, in James, A. & James, A. L. (eds) *European Childhoods: Cultures, Politics and Participation.* Basingstoke, England: Palgrave Macmillan

Nilsen, R. D. 2011, Flexible Spaces – Flexible Subjects in Nature. Transcending the Fenced Childhood in Daycare Centres? in Kjørholt, A.-T. & Qvortrup, J. (eds) *The Modern Child and the Flexible Labour Market: Early Childhood Education and Care.* Basingstoke: Palgrave Macmillan

Schiller, Pam, 2009, The Intentional Teacher, January/February Exchange magazine

Peacock, A. 2007, Using without using up: Involving teachers, children and communities in sustainable lifestyles, in Austin, R. (ed.) *Letting the Outside in: Developing Teaching And Learning Beyond the Early Years Classroom.* Stoke on Trent.: Trentham Books Limited

Piaget, 1972, Book title: Play and Development: A Symposium with Contributions by Jean Piaget, Peter H. Wolff and Others, Editor: Maria W. Piers, Article title: Some Aspects of Operations, Article author: Jean Piaget, Start Page 15, Quote Page 27, Published by W. W. Norton & Company, New York.

Pyle, Robert, 2002,. Eden in a Vacant Lot: Special Places, Species and Kids in Community of Life. In: Children and Nature: Psychological, Sociocultural and Evolutionary Investigations. Kahn, P.H. and Kellert, S.R. (eds) Cambridge: MIT Press

Plato, http://www.positivityblog.com/index.php/2007/04/20/21-inspirational-quotes-on-education/

Ryan, R. M., Weinstein, N., Bernstein, J., Brown, K. W., Mistretta, L., Gagné, M. 2010, Vitalizingeffects of ebing outdoors and in nature. Journal of Environmental Psychology, 30(2), 159–68

Sandseter, E. B. H. 2009a, Affordances for risky play in preschool: The importance of features in the play environment. *Early Childhood Education Journal*, 36(5), 439–46

Sandseter, E. B. H. 2009b, Characteristics of risky play. *Journal of Adventure Education & Outdoor Learning*, 9(1), 3–21

Sandseter, E. B. H. 2009c, Children's Expressions of Exhilaration and Fear in Risky Play. *Contemporary Issues in Early Childhood*, 10(2), 92–106

Sandseter, E. B. H., Little, H. & Wyver, S. 2012, Do theory and pedagogy have an impact on provisions for outdoor learning? A comparison of approaches in Australia and Norway. *Journal of Adventure Education & Outdoor Learning*, 12(3), 167–182

Sandseter, E. 2011, Children's risky play from an evolutionary perspective. *Evolutionary Psychology*, 9, 257–84

Scottish Government. (2012) 'Learning for Sustainability: The Report of the One Planet Schools Working Group'

Shipley, D. 2008, *Empowering Children: Play-based Curriculum for Lifelong Learning* (4th edn). USA: Nelson Education

Sobel, D. 1990, A Place in the World: Adults' Memories of Childhood's Special Places. *Children's Environments Quarterly*, 7(4), 5–12

Sobel, D. 1994, *Children's Special Places*. Tucson, AZ: Zephyr Press

Sobel, D. 2012, Look, Don't Touch. The problem with environmental education. *Leave No Child Inside*, July/August issue of *Orion* magazine

Look, Don't Touch, by DAVID SOBEL Orion Magazine > EducationJuly/August2012 https://orionmagazine.org/article/look-dont-touch1/

Storli, R. & Hagen, T. L. 2010, Affordances in outdoor environments and children's physically active play in pre-school. *European Early Childhood Education Research Journal*, 18(4), 445–56

Sunbury Gerber, L. 2014, www.regardingbaby.org/2010/09/20/no-tummy-time-necessary/

Swarbrick, N. Eastwood, G. Tutton, K. Self-esteem and successful interaction as part of the forest school project 2004

Taylor, A. F. & Kuo, F. E. 2009, Children with attention deficits concentrate better after walk in the park. *Journal of Attention Disorders*, 12(5), 402–9

Taylor, A. F., Kuo, F. E. & Sullivan, W. C. 2001, Coping with ADD The surprising connection to green play settings. *Environment and Behavior*, 33(1), 54–77

Tranter, P 2005, November, Strategies for building child friendly cities. Paper presented at the Creating Child Friendly Cities Conference, Melbourne. Retrieved June 2006, www.envict.org.au/file/Paul_Tranter.pdf

Tovey, H. 2007, *Playing Outdoors*. Open University Press

Winnicott, D. W., *Playing and Reality* p 54. Routeledge. 1971

Vize, Anne 2013, *Inclusive Outdoor Play*, Teaching Solutions

Waite, S. 2011, *Children Learning Outside the Classroom: From Birth to Eleven*. Sage Publications

Waite, S., Bølling, M. and Bentsen, P. 2015 Comparing apples and pears?: a conceptual framework for understanding forms of outdoor learning through comparison of English Forest Schools and Danish udeskole *Environmental Education Research*

Walsh, D. 2005, Developmental theory, in Yelland, N. (ed.) *Critical Issues In Early Childhood Education*. Berkshire, England: McGraw-Hill Education

Warden, C.H. 2012, *Nature Kindergartens and Forest Schools*. Mindstretchers

Wells, Nancy M. & Evans, Gary W. 2003, Nearby nature: A buffer of life stress among rural children. *Environment and Behavior*, 35(3), 311–30

White, J., Ellis, F., O'Malley, A., Rockel, J., Stover, S. & Toso, M. 2008, Play and Learning in Aotearoa New Zealand Early Childhood Education, in Samuelsson, I. P. & Fleer, M. (eds) *Play and Learning in Early Childhood Settings: International Perspectives*. Springer

Williams-Siegfredsen, J. 2012, *Understanding the Danish Forest Schools Approach*. London: Routledge

Wilson, Edward O. 1984, *Biophilia*, Cambridge: Harvard University Press

Useful websites

Children and Nature Network
www.childrenandnature.org

Forestry Commission
Information about adders.
www.forestry.gov.uk/forestry/adder

Nature Action Collaborative for Children
www.worldforumfoundation.org/working-groups/nature

Public Health England, Ticks and Your Health, Information about tick bite risks and prevention © Crown copyright 2016
https://www.gov.uk/government/uploads/system/uploads/attachment_data/file/504978/TSS_ticks_and_your_health.pdf

The United Nations Convention on the Rights of the Child
www.unicef.org.uk

Biography

Niki Buchan is an Educational Consultant with Natural Learning Early Childhood Consultancy. She has a biomedical background, is originally from South Africa, lived in Scotland for many years and has been calling Australia home since 2011. Niki has a great love for the outdoors and has been working with both adults and young children in very consultative, naturalistic and sensorial environments both indoors and outdoors for 35 years.

She works internationally as a conference keynote speaker, nature pedagogue, naturalistic playground advisor, international study visit facilitator, mentor and author, and she also delivers a large range of professional learning opportunities on all aspects of early child care and development.

Niki lived and worked in the UK for many years where she trained as a Forest School Leader. She was head of Morrison's Academy Nursery, recognised as a Centre of Excellence, worked with Claire Warden delivering keynote speeches and Early Years training, leading an action research project, co-authoring books and establishing one of the first Nature Kindergartens. Under Niki's headship these attained the highest possible status from HMIE (Her Majesty's Inspectorate of Education) in Scotland.

She was delighted to be offered a position in Australia, where she has developed a reputation as a strong advocate for children's right to a high-quality childhood, including having regular access to nature and having their voices heard. She is considered a leading voice in promoting nature-based practice internationally and is the author of *Children in Wild Nature*, written for Australia and now adapted for the UK. She is an adventurer and a keen photographer and is seldom seen without a camera in her hand.

Chapter 7 author biographies

Sarah MacQuarrie is a lecturer in the psychology of education at the Manchester Institute of Education, University of Manchester. Her research is focused on the application of psychology in education. Sarah is a Chartered Psychologist and Associate Fellow of the British Psychological Society.

Clare Nugent is a doctoral candidate at the University of Edinburgh. Following a PGCE in outdoor education, Clare taught in both the state and private sectors before a move to Scotland. She received her MEd in early childhood education from the University of Edinburgh in 2007 and is now completing her PhD; a comparative account of three case studies of Nature Kindergartens in Denmark, Finland and Scotland. The aim of this research is to better understand nature-based practice as constructed in different socio-cultural contexts.

Demonstrating the skill of lighting a fire using a fire steel before Niki supported these curious young children at Riverside Cottage Nursery in trying to light a fire themselves.